I0474420

Towards a Strategic Blend in Education

A review of the blended learning literature

Royce Willis (Lead Author)

Tony Yeigh

David Lynch

Richard Smith

Steve Provost

David Turner

Ken Sell

2018

Towards a Strategic Blend in Education: A review of the blended learning literature.

Copyright © 2018 Aoba Japan International School

National Library of Australia Cataloguing-in-Publication entry

Creator: Willis, Royce, lead author.

Title: Towards a strategic blend in education: a review of the blended learning literature / Royce Willis [and five] others.

ISBN: 9780244025748 (paperback)

Other authors: Tony Yeigh, David Lynch, Richard Smith, Steve Provost, David Turner, Ken Sell.

Subjects: Blended learning. Literature, Modern--Study and teaching (Higher)

**First Published in 2018
by Oxford Global Press
Kemp House
152 City Road, London (UK)**
www.oxfordglobal.com

 These works have been peer reviewed.

These works are a review of literature commissioned by:

Aoba Japan International School

7-5-1 Hikarigaoka, Nerima-ku, Tokyo 179-0072
https://www.japaninternationalschool.com

The works were compiled and written by **Southern Cross University**
CHEC, Hogbin Drive, Coffs Harbour, Australia.
www.scu.edu.au

Contents

About the Authors

Royce Willis (Lead Author)

Royce Willis is a researcher office with Southern Cross University. Royce has a background in Psychological Science, experienced in teaching at a tertiary level; online, face-to-face, and in blended modes. Currently a PhD candidate, Royce's research journey continues to develop, spanning psychology, statistics, environmental psychology, and education. Royce's background allows him to take a scientific approach to reading and writing about Blended Learning. He is involved in various funded research projects across the globe all focused on teaching improvement.

Dr Tony Yeigh

Tony Yeigh is a research academic and lecturer in the areas of educational psychology, classroom management and inclusive education at Southern Cross University, Australia. He is also leader of the Learning Sciences Research Group and an associate researcher with the Teacher Education Research Group, the Centre for Children & Young People, and the Association for Mindfulness in Education. Dr Yeigh has a keen interest in Blended Learning research, as it seeks to integrate a disruptive learning paradigm into traditional education.

Professor David Lynch

David Lynch is Professor of Education in the School of Education at Southern Cross University. He is the author of numerous articles and texts on whole of school reform, teaching improvement, teacher education and related matters and one of Australia's foremost teacher education innovators. His research and development interests form the basis of a radical rethink on teaching, whole of school teaching reform and teacher education and these are reflected in his seminal published works over the past twenty years. He has had a distinguished academic career at several universities in Australia, having held a number of senior academic leadership positions, and consults in education jurisdictions across the globe.

Emeritus Professor Richard Smith

Emeritus Professor Richard Smith has extensive experience in administering and governing education institutions and dealing with state and federal education bureaucracies. He has a distinguished record in research, publication and postgraduate supervision. His academic and applied interests lie in the reform and development of teaching theory and pedagogical practice at all levels, social policy development and governance in education. Richard has a long association with international education, cultural exchanges and collaboration and has a special relationship with several higher education institutions in China at both college and elite research levels.

Dr Steven Provost

Steve Provost teaches experimental psychology, behaviour analysis and methodology in the School of Health and Human Sciences at Southern Cross University. He has published work in learning, human factors and psychopharmacology. More recently, the focus of his research interests has been in teaching and learning in higher education. He received the Australian Psychological Society's Award for Distinguished Contribution to Psychology Education in 2010. He was a member of the team of authors responsible for the publication of an Australian and NZ edition of Doug Bernstein's introductory text "Psychology: An International Discipline in Context".

Dr David Turner

David Turner is Director of Professional Learning for the Queensland Association of State School Principals. He is a former Head of School of Education at Central Queensland University and State School (primary) principal in Queensland, Australia. Dr Turner has published articles in the areas of teacher education, teaching improvement and the teaching school concept and is works as a conjoint association professor at Southern Cross University focusing on research into whole of school teaching improvement.

Ken Sell

Ken Sell is the Head of Aoba-Japan International School in Japan and is presently engaged in a school based project designed to support the Japanese national education system reform agenda. He is an adjunct of Southern Cross University. Having previously held educational leadership positions in Australia, Norway and China, Ken's research is informed by his innovate approaches to leadership and the building of professional capital in schools. Starting with his work for Central Queensland University (CQU), where he developed the unique Noosa Hub's Master of Learning Management program, he has continued to investigate and publish research and articles related to the practical application of investing in 'teachers as researchers', 'receptive accountability' and 'professional capital' in schools. As a reflective practitioner, who has worked in diverse educational settings, Ken has dedicated his career to supporting school and teacher transformation.

Foreword

Iwao Shibata-san
Professor, Graduate School of Management, Business Breakthrough University
Board Chair, Aoba-Japan International School

We now live in a world where the 'global flow' of goods, services, finances, people, ideas, and data is estimated to triple by 2025. Among other things, digitization is transforming and enriching this flow to a point not yet fully understood. A report by McKinsey and Company (2014) called 'Global flows in a digital age: How trade, finance, people, and data connect the world economy' makes for interesting reading. It points out that in today's world global flows are growing and increasingly contribute to world GDP growth. There has been an 18-fold increase in cross border internet traffic between 2005 and 2012. The growth in the trade of knowledge intensive goods is 1.3 x faster than labor-intensive goods. A 500% increase in Skype call minutes since 2008 is seemingly incomprehensible. 90% of sellers on eBay export to other countries. Entrepreneurs have more opportunities to participate in cross-border exchanges than ever before.

For many this digitized world is no longer a just a 'virtual world' it is their 'real world'. One just has to spend a little time analyzing what is happening in China, India and Africa to realise this new digitized world is not limited to the established economies of the world. In today's 'real world' the entrepreneur and small businesses are becoming "micro-multinationals". Digitization gives them the capacity to sell and source products, provide services from a distance, and move ideas across borders.

But what does this mean for schooling and education? Put simply, since the advent of powerful search engines such as Google, we have seen a fundamental change in education. How we treat knowledge and the teacher-learner relationship has come under increasing scrutiny. Although the past industrial model of education was robust and, in part, got us to where we are now, it is becoming increasingly irrelevant. The industrial model, in other words the old model of schooling, focused on input: it was all about how knowledge is acquired most efficiently by the largest number of students. In contrast, the new model of education to emerge as one response to our digitized world focusses on output. This new model is about facilitating how 'learners' best gather and apply knowledge with a positive purpose in mind.

In the new digitized model, we are witnessing ICT replacing the hard copy text book and the pen as essential tools. Learning in real life is replacing the 'just in case' learning that is bound by classroom walls, the teacher as the centre of attention and a seemingly rigid and increasingly irrelevant curriculum. Teachers are now adopting a pedagogy characterized by facilitation, support and differentiation, replacing the one-size-fits-all pedagogy. We are increasingly seeing the evaluation of learning in terms of how learners define a question and then set about answering it. This is in contrast to the 'old model' of evaluation that asks the student to find the right answer.

These changes are happening not because any particular government or authorities decided, but because our society and businesses have changed as such. This being the case, it is incumbent on schools to adjust accordingly. One of the major missions of today's school's educational institutions is to support learners to be prepared for the 'real world'. In other words, a school should respond and account for the real changes occurring in our world today.

Clearly, the comparison between the old world and new world gives us insight into the direction our education institutions should go. This book is an important contribution to providing the educational community with supporting research to help inform change. It came about through an ongoing collaboration between Aoba-Japan International School (A-JIS), Southern Cross

University (SCU), and Business Breakthrough University (BBTU) to support their mutual commitment to develop a global-standard, blended, and inquiry-based learning curriculum and platform.

In this collaboration, A-JIS has led in the development of the conceptual model, the trialing of new pedagogies, and the design and development of a bespoke learning platform to support the endeavor. SCU has provided crucial research and data analysis, teacher training, and impartial observational feedback to the A-JIS leadership team. BBT University provided its proprietary online learning platform as the base from which the new bespoke K-12 platform has been developed. This collaboration and research is very unique; it is only feasible by a team comprising those three disparate areas of expertise: a K-12 IB World School, a university with in-depth expertise in education and pedagogy, and in-depth expertise in e-learning and related technologies. As this collaboration continues, using the newly-developed content and blended-learning curriculum in a real school setting in A-JIS hands-on findings in this field will be further examined.

By examining the contemporary literature associated with the intersection between ICT and learning in schools, this book provides educational leaders and teachers with valuable insights into the state of play at the moment. It is designed as point of reference to inform decision making by those who are deeply committed to changing the direction of schools and other educational institutions so they reflect the current new world context.

Executive Summary

It is the purpose of this literature review to clarify the role, purpose and nature of *Blended Learning* as an emerging pedagogical approach. The term Blended Learning (BL) is used to refer to a particular pedagogy that combines the use of online technology with more traditional instructional strategies, in order to provide a more engaging approach for student learning. At the heart of BL lies the notion that effective teaching and learning, as connected to modern technology, requires teachers to relinquish control over the teaching/learning process, in order to allow for more student-focused and student-directed learning to occur.

There exists no overall agreement concerning an operational definition for BL, yet there is a broad consensus that it includes some mixture of online and face-to-face (F2F) instructional strategies, designed to operate in a complimentary fashion. This quite broad definition can be clarified somewhat by the additional suggestions made by Staker (2011), Staker and Horn (2012) and Christensen, Horn, and Staker (2013), denoting that BL should be implemented as a formal education program, include some element of student control and provide an integrated learning experience. However, the emerging nature of BL as a pedagogical approach actually lends itself to the development of multiple "working definitions", in order to provide the flexibility required to apply the concept across a variety of different applied and research foci. Thus the broader, somewhat vague definition of BL - as consisting of some F2F teaching and some online teaching - appears appropriate to the current state of BL development, allowing as it does flexible implementation of the pedagogy at a school-based level. Ongoing definitional development to assist BL clarity include:

1. Use of an initial working definition to aid the application of BL to the immediate context of interest, providing sufficient detail to allow for replication of the methods used to aid future applications and research.

2. Use of the broad, umbrella term to aid discussion about BL, in order not to restrict general discussion of BL to a definition which obscures or eliminates parts of the continuum or partial implementation.

3. Ensuring that the definition functions to support the effectiveness of BL in relation to learning. Thus, any definition of BL which reduces freedom to improve education should be avoided.

Models of BL

Although the essential definition relating to Blended Learning (BL) can be represented as a bi-polar continuum, involving F2F and Online, the application of this continuum to teaching and learning requires the consideration of multiple factors that also impact on the nature of BL, including the type of interactivity involved (synchronous/asynchronous), whether the learning is collaborative or individual, self-paced or scheduled, involves a face-to-face or face-to-screen format, is teacher-focused or student-focused, and involves active-learning or passive-learning. These additional elements are then incorporated into BL in relation to the purpose and scope of the BL application, creating a diversity of BL models at the level of implementation.

These models range from the more basic (*Face-to-Face Driver* or *Supplementary* model, involving largely F2F onsite learning, with supplemental online aspects), to more complex models (such as the *Replacement model*, which replaces F2F time with some form of online or e-learning). Of interest, the Replacement Model can be further iterated according to the degree to which it requires changes to facilities and/or staff for implementation, with minimal change requirements viewed as a *sustaining* iteration (e.g., Station Rotation, Lab Rotation, and Flipped Classroom) and major change requirements viewed as a *disrupting* iteration (Flex Model, A La Carte Model, Individual Rotation, and the Enriched Virtual Model). Thus, the degree to which any given model of BL disrupts F2F teaching and learning arrangements forms a basic principle of model differentiation. Research concerning model efficacy has yet to sufficiently delineate the efficiency of disruption at his early stage of BL development, but this research does support the underlying definition of BL at a general level, by emphasising the need to design BL implementation from a "needs-based" perspective that is appropriate to the goals, purpose and context of the school and situation of interest.

Blended Learning Elements

Taking this needs-based perspective into account, applying Blended Learning (BL) to individual schools and education systems involves considering BL dimensions and some specific elements of BL. Dimensional considerations include *Reach* (the breadth of the BL program), *School Type* (public, private, etc.), *Operational Control* (level of governance for the program), *Grade Level* (the elements and extent of BL being implemented into different grade levels), *Comprehensiveness* (degree of integration across school courses), *Location* (primary placement of the BL program), and *Type of Instruction* (where along the F2F – Online continuum will the program be positioned?). Related to type of instruction are the dimensions of *Teacher-Student Interaction* and *Student-Student Interaction*, which both have to do with the type and style of communication students will have with the teacher and with one another. In relation to communication, the dimension of *Delivery* has to do with whether these interactions will be synchronous (the interactions occur in real time, e.g., video conferencing) or asynchronous (interactions do not occur in real time, e.g., online discussion boards, email), with both forms of delivery often included within a single BL program. As an aspect of BL delivery, it is important to note that synchronous interactions appear to better promote cooperation and collaboration amongst students, while asynchronous interactions appear to better promote student focussed and self-directed learning.

Specific Elements of BL

Web 2.0 Tools

There are a number of additional elements that support or compliment the use of BL, including web 2.0 tools, blogs, podcasts, and vodcasts. Understanding the role and function of these elements is also necessary for understanding how to design and implement a successful BL program or approach, so a discussion of them is included in the review.

Specific use of web 2.0 tools (social networking programs characterised by the way they allow for user input; e.g. Twitter, Flickr, YouTube, Facebook) can be used to allow students to add content which can then be viewed by others. These tools can be highly interactive (Twitter or Facebook) or allow for more reflective, asynchronous interactions (Flickr or Facebook). Web 2.0 tools offer important support for BL because they are effective at promoting self-directed learning on the part of students, for example:

- Although not highly interactive, blogs can be used to support BL in that they are easy to use, self-directed and allow students to submit and update their work in real-time. They also allow students to reflect on course content in a less formal way than more traditional assignment formats such as an essay. Teachers can provide clear direction for blogs by providing initial content, and this has been found to be an effective way to promote student reflection, collaboration and interactivity.
- A highly interactive 2.0 tool is Twitter, a social networking platform that allows students to exchange information and ideas with one another - and worldwide if needed - at a rapid pace that is almost instantaneous. Twitter accounts can be set up and deleted as necessary too, making this particular tool extremely flexible in terms

of its application across different learning groups and situations. Because of these "now" characteristics, Twitter has proven effective in increasing student engagement.

- Podcasts and vodcasts (audio and video recordings, such as YouTube utilises) form a set of tools that are good for promoting student self-direction. When used judiciously, these particular tools are believed to assess learning more deeply than written assignments.

Online Quizzes

Assessment feedback is very important for students, and online quizzes support this process by allowing ongoing asynchronous access to tests that can automatically mark student results and provide immediate feedback. The use of online quizzes in conjunction with a Flipped Classroom Model of BL appears particularly well-suited to improved student outcomes, as well as making the learning more enjoyable for students.

Digital Games and Virtual Worlds

Digital games and virtual worlds represent technologies that offer more imaginable possibilities for teaching and learning than many other technologies normally associated with BL. Digital games that have been created or modified for educational use appear notably effective for producing positive student outcomes across a range of learning areas. Virtual worlds provide engaging online simulation environments, where the student can interact with elements of the online environment in a goal-oriented manner designed to achieve specific learning outcomes. Caveats attached to the educational use of these technologies include scepticism on the part of both teachers and students, as well as the need for relevant training in the technology prior to its implementation.

Automated Guidance

Automated guidance refers to computerised instructional programs that are able to give students specific, step-by-step guidance through learning tasks in a way that scaffolds for pre-determined outcomes and levels of learning at a pace best suited to the student. These programs can be used to promote mastery of a given topic or task, and are able to deliver corrective feedback as required. The use of automated guidance has proven especially relevant to learning in the STEM and other science-based areas, and for use with students who have lower levels of content knowledge. It thus provides one way of offering individualised learning across the diverse range of differences that often occurs within a school, classroom or group of learners.

Learning Management System

A learning management system (LMS) is essentially an online course management system used to create the virtual learning environment within which a BL program is embedded. The LMS thus represents a core technology that can be used to support a BL approach, and if implemented can be used to control accessibility, course content, course communication, regulation of learning, the use of software and tools, and the collection of program data. This might sound comprehensive, but the use of a LMS is not always required, and considerations concerning the scope, nature, and intentions of the BL program need to be made before this decision could move forward. Indeed, whether or not to incorporate a LMS into the BL design is fundamental to the overall development of any given BL, and as such requires consideration of costs, availability of technical support, and the degree to which the BL program might need to be customised for specific application. This decision, perhaps more than any other BL design element, emphasises the imperative to take a needs-based approach to the set-up and implementation of an individual BL program for a school, school system, or other educational setting.

Emerging Technologies

As the modern mobile phone continues to be the centre of technology integration within most societies, the emergence of various mobile technologies that are capable of being integrated with mobile phone use, or which have direct internet connection themselves, is paving the way for yet another wave of additional elements that can be, or could be, applied within a BL program. These technologies tend to be quite "cutting-edge" in terms of development, however, and because of this we cover their suggested use at the level of projected BL support, more than at the level of specific implementation, within the constraints of this literature review.

Student Outcomes

There exists limited research investigating the relationship between BL and student achievement, yet we note that student outcomes lie at the heart of all considerations concerning the design and implementation of a given BL program or approach. In this respect it is important to understand that an initial "teething" period, involving both student and teacher familiarisation with the elements of BL from an educational perspective, is to be expected when a new BL program is put into place. Any expectation, therefore, that implementing a new BL program is going to result in immediate improved outcomes for students should be avoided on the basis that program familiarisation must occur first.

Looking beyond this initial learning curve, most of the extant research on BL use in schools (K – 12) has shown the use of BL to have a positive effect on student outcomes, and specific training concerning the educational use of the BL elements or tools, coupled to the provision of a clear rationale as to why students are being asked to use them in this way, seems to shorten the length of time for the student familiarisation learning curve. This helps to personalise the BL program, thereby increasing student control over their learning and providing greater self-direction and ownership of the learning. In this respect knowing how to strike a balance between teacher control and student self-regulation will be a core consideration for the design of a BL program, and some discussion regarding how to assist students to develop self-regulated learning skills is provided in this part of our review.

Social interaction is also an important factor for student engagement, having a notable effect on student outcomes, and in this respect the positioning of a BL program along the F2F – BL continuum represents another crucial balance that must be considered as part of the BL design. Too much online learning decreases the opportunities for social interaction, but too much F2F learning decreases the opportunities for student self-regulation. Educational learning involves strong socialisation aspects, which act to motivate greater engagement overall. Because of this, it is important to design BL in a way that promotes a high degree of social interaction, and we discuss strategies for doing this as part of the literature review.

Overall, it appears that program flexibility, variation of presentation mode, greater student control, quick feedback, the provision of social interaction, and the ability to individualise learning all encourage greater student engagement in BL programs. In turn, these elements encourage and promote improved student outcomes over time. They are also viewed as integral to lifelong learning, in that the development of information and technological literacy increases learner confidence and digital competence, as well as promoting an ability to work independently, all of which have also been linked to better outcomes at tertiary levels of learning.

Teacher Professional Development

There are many benefits, it seems, that stem from a BL design that is appropriate to the intended purpose and goals of an educational program, and the inclusion of elements specific to teacher Professional Development (PD) extends these benefits to the teachers themselves. Working within a BL program, teachers are able to undertake PD remotely and via asynchronous involvement if needed. The use of external professionals, expert in particular BL elements, can also work through the program as part of the PD process. Using BL to learn about BL is at the centre of this sort of PD, and the inclusion of data collection relevant to the PD process will be necessary to measure the effects of the training successfully. This is especially important in light of the existing research concerning BL and PD, as most of this research has taken place at the anecdotal level of investigation. It is obvious, therefore, that a clear need for more rigorous research in this area is required. In this respect it has been found that focussing too much on implementation and not enough on evaluation has been found to hinder the transition to BL.

The focus for PD needs to be on the relationships between curriculum content, syllabus outcomes, instructional pedagogy, and technological delivery, and we provide a discussion of TPACK (*Technological Pedagogical And Content Knowledge*) and the *Blended Learning Teacher Competency Framework*, as well as other training models, to detail this focus area more clearly. Understanding how to provide PD specifically aimed at covering the additional elements of teaching and learning that are imposed by technology allows teachers to not only master the relevant content, pedagogy, and technology required, but to also understand how to integrate the pedagogy and technology appropriately within a given discipline. This therefore presents as a foundational BL knowledge area, and one that will continue to evolve over time, as new technologies are created and become available for incorporation into the BL framework.

Implementing Blended Learning

This section of the literature review provides some guidance concerning how to implement BL into schools and other educational settings. Many schools begin their experience of BL by piloting a BL course first, to assess how it affects student engagement and learning. We note, however, that eight levels of "eLearning readiness" have been suggested as a means for determining the degree to which a school or school system is capable of implementing BL, including *Environmental Readiness*, *Cultural Readiness*, *Management Readiness*, *Personnel Readiness*, *Learner Readiness*, *Financial Readiness*, *Technical Readiness*, and *Content Readiness*. The degree of readiness for these eLearning areas can be used to help decide the extent of BL implementation that will take place in a school, but there are additional factors that also impact on readiness, such as school leadership, staff attitudes, availability and extent of PD for the program, and the initial scope and goals of the program.

Initial decisions about the implementation of BL will need to determine whether to use a sustaining innovation model or a disruptive innovation model as the basis BL approach. This would require an autonomous team within the school, including members with technical expertise, to begin the conversion process. The use of a selective group of students to participate in the program, perhaps a specific group of struggling students or some advanced students, could then be used to assist program adjustments and refine it until effective. Once the program is consistent and effective, it can be expanded to other courses in the school.

Regardless of program scope, early decisions concerning the BL approach include the identification of clear goals and objectives, the capacity of the school or organisation to design and implement BL courses successfully, costs of design and implementation, clear operational definitions concerning program concepts and principles (and clear criteria for evaluating these), the nature and extent of technical support for the program, the provision of appropriate infrastructure for the program, the possible need for legal advice and/or policy development, the particular course objectives involved, which models – and elements - of BL to provide for the different grades involved, and how to rationalise the relationships that exist between program content, pedagogy and the technology involved. Thus, extensive forethought, good planning, and design are all pre-requisite to the design of a successful BL program.

Limitations and Gaps in the Research

The relationship between BL implementation and BL research is one of reciprocity, wherein implementation is capable of providing information and data for research in the area, while research acts as a means of documenting, interpreting, and advancing BL knowledge. In this respect we note there are significant limitations and gaps in the BL research literature, including that a dearth of research seems to have been performed in this area, that the research which has been performed often lacks rigour, that the literature often contains poor descriptions of the research irrespective of its rigour, that the research has tended to utilise inconsistent research methods, that there is a lack of clear data from the research, and that little dissemination of research findings has occurred.

Research rigour and dissemination of the research are extremely important if we want knowledge around BL to advance at a faster pace, and we note that for both research and dissemination this needs to include how student learning is being affected by the BL program involved. To this end we discuss the need to design quality research as a means of contributing to the success of individual BL implementations, as well as to the BL field in general, toward the end of the review, and include specific recommendations concerning how to approach the research design process.

Blended Learning: A Review of Literature

Blended Learning (BL), in its most basic definition, is the blending of online, external education and onsite, traditional education. When done right, BL should incorporate the best of each mode, and design-out the least useful aspects of each mode. Research to date has shown that, overall, BL can lead to improved student outcomes (Bernard et al., 2014; Florida TaxWatch, 2007; Means, Toyama, Murphy, & Baki, 2013; Poon, 2013; Schmid et al., 2014). However, being a relatively new field, there are many questions surrounding best practices in implementing, designing, and teaching BL. This is perhaps due to a lack of clarity in its definition, a lack of quality and quantity in its research, or simply due to BLs vastness. Most likely, it is a product of all of these things, and probably a multitude of other reasons.

This literature review was intended to identify evidence-based strategies for implementing, designing, and teaching BL in K-12 education, with a focus on improving student outcomes. However, strong evidence was found to be lacking in each of these areas. Thus, instead, the scope of this literature review had to be broadened to include evidence from purely online education, from tertiary education, and from anecdotal evidence. Although not ideal, this is the current stage of BLs progression. Developing evidence-based best practices for BL could be looked upon as an overwhelming and impossible challenge, and indeed it is a great task. Alternatively, it could be viewed as an exciting and ripe area of research, waiting for capable, pioneering researchers to forge a way through. With the latter focus in mind, this literature review is intended to identify what is known, identify where gaps in evidence are, and give direction to future research and implementation of BL.

Although there are vast gaps in the BL literature, there is also some good evidence which should form the basis of future BL research. This literature review endeavours to highlight some of this research and pave the way for a new era of quality research in BL. Initially, a definition of BL will be discussed. This will allow for clear communication on the topic. From there, some existing BL models and potential technological elements will be detailed. Although not exhaustive, these sections identify current examples of how BL is being used. This will be followed by a section on student outcomes; what has worked and what should be included to improve student outcomes in BL. What is required to be effective BL teachers is then discussed. This includes general and theoretical considerations, but also potential methods for BL professional development. Strategies and considerations for implementing BL into a school will then be considered. This includes aspects of planning and considerations of the school's readiness for BL implementation. Finally, what is lacking and what is needed in BL research will be addressed. Overall, it is hoped that this literature review will give those new to BL a clear picture of the state of BL at this time and direction to pursue its implementation, but also to consolidate this information for those already familiar with BL, potentially giving direction to future research.

Defining Blended Learning

A definition of Blended Learning (BL) has not been widely agreed upon. Agreement is extended to BL having some portion in an online environment, and some portion in a traditional face-to-face (F2F) bricks-and-mortar environment (Graham, 2012). However, this

25

is where the agreement ends. This section will give a brief overview of some attempts at defining BL, concluding with suggestions for future definition use.

One method for separating these methods into classes ranging from traditional teaching to fully online teaching, is to assess the percentages of each method used. This, in effect, would create a continuum of teaching methods available. For example, Allen, Seaman, and Garrett (2007) suggest that *Traditional* learning consists of 0% online, including 1-29% would be regarded as *Web-facilitated* learning, 30-79% of online learning would be defined as *BL*, and *Fully Online* learning would have 80-100% of instruction in an online format. At first glance this may seem like a clear and concise method for defining the teaching method involved, but it is not clear where these numbers have been derived. Is one or two percent difference in online instruction really what we should base efforts to develop efficient and effective BL courses on? For example, if we were tasked with developing a BL course and found that the most effective teaching model consisted of just 29% online instruction, would it be appropriate to add an extra 1% to fit the definition despite the reduction in effectiveness? Although the percentage of online instruction may serve as a vague guide, it is not recommended to strictly adhere to arbitrary percentages as the basis upon which to define BL (Department of Education and Early Childhood Development, 2012).

Dziuban, Hartman, and Moskal (2004) suggest that BL is simply any combination of F2F and online learning. However, they do specify that the online content should replace F2F content, not merely be added to it. They go on to explain that each element should be used to its strengths, reducing the weaknesses of the other. Although this definition is less restrictive than the use of percentage cut-offs, there are yet two points to consider. Firstly, a strict one-to-one replacement of F2F with online learning will place unnecessary restrictions on the definition of BL similar to the percentage cut-offs. Would a course still be BL if it added 15% more online content while reducing F2F by 10%? Should supplementary material not be available online because more F2F would need to be replaced? While it may be recommended to reduce F2F when introducing online elements, so as not to overload students, this should not be strictly enforced as a one-to-one exchange. The corollary of this is that if it is not a strict requirement of BL, it should not be included in the definition.

Our second point involves Dziuban, Hartman, and Moskal's (2004) assertion that suggestions of maintaining the strengths while reducing the weaknesses of F2F and online elements is something to aspire to, not necessarily a fundamental element of BL. In a similar manner Graham (2012) suggests the same of Picciano's (2009) inclusion of "planned, pedagogically valuable manner" (p. 8) as a required element of BL. Thus, these notions can be seen more as aspirational guides for "best practice" BL, rather than as the necessary elements of a definition.

Heather Staker and her colleagues developed a definition of BL over several years. The original definition was:

> Blended learning is any time a student learns at least in part at a supervised brick- and-mortar location away from home and at least in part through online delivery with some element of student control over time, place, path, and/or pace (Staker, 2011, p. 5).

This definition basically clarifies what is generally agreed upon as BL; a combination of F2F and online learning. The addition of student control is perhaps unnecessary, as it may be assumed, but it does not reduce the effectiveness of the definition. In a subsequent paper, Staker and Horn (2012) suggested that BL must also be "a formal education program" (p. 4), to exclude, for example, students playing educational computer games in their own time as forming the online part of BL. They also suggest that the definition include "online delivery of content and instruction" (p. 4), to clarify that mere online browsing by students at home does not constitute as the online element of BL, even if it is relevant to the course. Christensen, Horn, and Staker (2013) then added that the F2F and online components should "provide an integrated learning experience" (p.7). These definitions were intentionally broad to allow for ongoing use as technology and methods advance, and did not include aspirational suggestions because BL can still be classified as BL regardless of its effectiveness (Staker & Horn, 2012). It might be argued that the most recent addition to the definition, provision of an "integrated learning experience" (Christensen, Horn, & Staker, 2013, p.7), is perhaps an aspirational suggestion. Because the effectiveness of this integration is not included, however, this argument can be dismissed.

The lack of an accepted definition can lead to confused empirical research, which, in turn, does not aid in developing a clear definition of BL (Philadelphia Education Research Consortium [PERC], 2014). However, there are a number of reasons why a more unified definition of BL is not apparent at this time. Firstly, BL is a new and developing field, and thus its definitional elements are still emerging. Secondly, specific working definitions of BL are often developed to suit the foci of research (Partridge, Ponting, & McCay, 2011), and although the use of a working definition is necessary to develop and test hypotheses, this has tended to encourage the development of multiple definitions, rather than a more unified definition. Another reason for the lack of a clear definition for BL is that it is an umbrella term which describes a continuum of methodologies (PERC, 2014). Thus, within its current state of development, trying to force a specific definition of BL may well reduce its utility in terms of authentically describing the pedagogical continuum it seeks to represent.

The general agreement that BL consists of some F2F teaching and some online teaching may seem too vague. However, if we consider why BL is being discussed at all, it becomes easier to see why we might view this definition as sufficient. A large part of the BL literature and discussion is intended to develop methods to efficiently and effectively educate students. Thus, a workable definition for BL will be one in which its school-based implementation allows the approach to develop freely, aspiring to educate students efficiently and effectively in a flexible and adaptive manner. In this respect a less restrictive definition for BL appears to be most useful, in that it allows for unrestricted innovation (Sharpe, Benfield, Roberts, & Francis, 2006).

To conclude, although a clear and concise definition has not been developed, here are some suggestions for ongoing definition development and use:

1. Use a working definition to aid the application of BL to the immediate context of interest, providing sufficient detail to allow for replication of the methods used to aid future applications and research.

2. Use the broad, umbrella term to aid discussion about BL in order to not restrict general discussion of BL to a definition which obscures or eliminates parts of the continuum.

3. Ensure that the definition functions to support the effectiveness of BL on learning. Any definition of BL which reduces freedom to improve education should be avoided.

Models

Using the umbrella term of BL, a number of models described in the BL literature will be described and discussed. As with the definition of BL, there is not a single model which has been found to be most effective in all situations. The unifying feature of these models is that they all fall somewhere along the BL continuum; somewhere between fully online and traditional learning (Watson, 2008).

The fully online to traditional learning is not the only continuum involved in BL. There are also considerations whether a course will have synchronous and asynchronous elements. That is, will the instructional arrangements be fully live and interactive (synchronous), or pre-recorded and otherwise available as required (asynchronous). Will the BL element be social, where students and/or staff can interact, or isolated, where the task is the students alone? Will it be onsite or offsite? Self-paced or scheduled? Face-to-face or face-to-screen? Teacher-focused or Student-focused? Active-learning or passive-learning? Individual or cooperative or collaborative? These aspects of BL all need to be considered, and require research in order to discover which is most effective in which courses. How some of the BL aspects are used will now be discussed, along with their use within some existing BL models.

Face-to-Face Driver model

The most basic, and perhaps primitive, form of BL is commonly known as the *Face-to-Face Driver Model* (Staker et al., 2011) or the *Supplementary Model* (Twigg, 2003). This consists of largely F2F onsite learning, with supplemental online aspects. In fact, this model may not be considered BL in some definitions because it does not necessarily replace F2F with online content (e.g. Dziuban, Hartman, & Moskal, 2004). The online elements may be available in the classroom, for example, in-class computer-based tutorials with immediate feedback which can be used for remediation for students when necessary (Staker et al., 2011; Twigg, 2003). Otherwise the supplementary content might be available offsite, for example, in the form of repeatable online quizzes which allow students to increase content knowledge (Twigg, 2003). This model allows students to take more time to learn content if necessary. Although this model has shown success (Twigg, 2003), it is generally recommended to redesign the course with online content incorporated, rather than simply adding supplementary online content (Dziuban, Hartman, & Moskal, 2004; Jimoyiannis, Tsiotakis, Roussinos, & Siorenta, 2013; Sharpe, Benfield, Roberts, & Francis, 2006).

Replacement Model

The next step on the continuum according to Twigg (2003), is the *Replacement Model*. As you may have guessed, this replaces time spent in traditional learning with some form of online or e-learning. This can, of course, take many forms. Staker et al. (2011) further defined a number of models which fit the Replacement Model definition, of which Christensen, Horn, and Staker (2013) further categorized into *sustaining* or *disruptive* innovations. These models will now be discussed, beginning with the sustaining models.

Sustaining Innovation Models

A brief explanation of a sustaining innovation in the context of BL is that it does not require major changes to facilities or staff (Christensen, Horn, & Staker, 2013). If the benefits of BL are to be fully recognized, however, courses should be redesigned, not merely upgraded with online content (Precel, Eshet-Alkalai, & Alberton, 2009; Twigg, 2003). This can be implemented within existing frameworks and physical locations, although teachers will likely require professional development. Christensen, Horn, and Staker (2013) describe the models Station Rotation, Lab Rotation, and Flipped Classroom as being sustaining innovations.

Station Rotation

Station Rotation consists of students rotating between online and F2F modalities within a subject (Christensen, Horn, & Staker, 2013; Staker & Horn, 2012). This much is true

31

of the four Rotation Models described by Staker and Horn (2012; Station Rotation, Lab Rotation, Flipped Classroom, and Individual Rotation), but the Station Rotation Model differs in that the rotation between modalities exists entirely within a brick-and-mortar classroom. This classroom is divided into stations which may include an area for traditional teacher-focused instruction, group-based work and discussion, one-to-one tutoring, and, of course, to classify as BL it requires an online component. The schedule of rotation may be teacher-allocated or a fixed time. Staker and Horn (2012) give an example of successful implementation of the Station Rotation Model where kindergarten students are rotated between computers, a small group collaboration station, and an instruction station, all within the same classroom. Although this will not suit all definitions of BL (because there is no offsite element), it may be an important first step for younger students in gaining an understanding of the technology and what is required of them. The Rotation Station Model can alleviate the burden of large class sizes on the teacher by breaking groups into smaller groups, with varying degrees of supervision required for each group (Walne, 2012). It is considered a sustaining innovation because, with the addition of some computers and some classroom reorganization, this model could easily be implemented into a previously traditional classroom.

Lab Rotation

Lab Rotation is much like the Station Rotation Model, but with the online component taking place outside of the classroom (Staker & Horn, 2012). The online component might occur in a computer lab or in the school library, or it might be taken at home or in a public library, for example. An example of successful implementation of Lab Rotation can be found at Rocketship schools in the USA (Rocketship, 2015). Here K-5 students are rotated into an online computer lab for two hours per day where they receive mathematics and reading instruction. The online computer program adapts to students, progressing faster for high achievers and allowing extra time when students are struggling. This is an example of how BL can provide individualised learning for students which would be very difficult to attain in large traditional classrooms. Although this model requires additional space for a computer lab or availability of an existing computer lab, it is still considered to be a sustaining innovation; able to be implemented into a traditional school without excessive facility or staff changes. There is evidence, however, that teachers are often not effectively linking the content of the F2F and online components to maximise learning (Walne, 2012), and this must be taken into consideration when evaluating the use of this particular model of BL.

Flipped Classroom

The *Flipped Classroom Model* (AKA Inverted Classroom) is considered to be a Rotation Model because it consists of rotation between in F2F classroom tasks and tasks to be performed in one's own time online. The major difference in the Flipped Classroom is that the tasks are somewhat reversed from what is traditionally expected (Lage, Platt, & Treglia, 2000). Lecture-style content is accessed outside of the traditional classroom, while what might have previously been considered homework-style activities are performed within the classroom. This model has been shown to increase student involvement and engagement levels (Clark, 2015). This model can also alleviate issues students may have with completing homework, instead allowing for repeated viewing of online content to increase learning (Walne, 2012). Stillwater Area Public Schools, Minnesota, has successfully implemented this model in grades 4-6 mathematics. Students view short asynchronous video and complete an online quiz. Online learning is then applied in the brick-and-mortar classroom. Flipped Classrooms are considered a sustaining innovation because it would require similar facilities as the Lab Rotation Model at most, potentially even less if students performed online tasks at home. Although there will be costs involved in establishing these sustaining innovation models within a traditional school, the overall framework of the school will be maintained and, with some professional development, staff will be able to continue within their more-or-less traditional roles.

Disruptive Innovation Models

We will now focus on the disruptive innovation models as described by Christensen, Horn, and Staker (2013). Disruptive innovation in regards to BL can be briefly described as requiring changes in facilities and staff. This does not mean there is no place for the existing teachers within the disruptive innovation models, but there will likely be role changes and potentially the addition of, for example, technical staff. Theoretically, a disruptive innovation model of BL could exist entirely outside of a traditional education framework. Christensen, Horn, and Staker (2013) describe the Flex Model, the A La Carte Model, the Individual Rotation Model, and the Enriched Virtual Model as being disruptive innovations.

Flex Model

The *Flex Model* is largely based online, although not necessarily offsite (Staker et al., 2011). Students, however, have access to onsite F2F interaction with teachers as required. The Flex Model gives some control over progress to the students; perhaps only enforcing cut-off dates for completion. An example of successful implementation of the Flex Model can be seen at AdvancePath Academics (AdvancePath Academics, n.d.; Christensen, Horn, & Staker, 2013). A typical facility consists of a 280 m^2 room divided into a computer lab, an offline area (for reading and writing), and a small group instruction area. Students are not allocated by age cohorts, as each works at their own pace with teacher intervention as required. Online programs guide students through milestones on their personal roadmap to graduation. Staff involved in the Flex Model include professional teachers, paraprofessionals, technical staff, and administration. This model can be seen as a disruptive innovation because it requires either major facility staff changes within an existing school, or it could even exist outside of a traditional school setting.

A La Carte Model

The *A La Carte Model* (AKA Self-Blend Model) is nearly entirely online, although it may be taken onsite (Staker & Horn, 2012). What differentiates this model from a fully online course is that it only includes certain courses within a school. That is, a school may offer online elective courses as a supplement to the general core subjects, or even offer some core subjects online, but students are still required to complete a portion of their schooling in a brick-and-mortar classroom. An example of the successful implementation of the A La Carte Model can be seen in Quakertown Community School District (Quakertown Community School District, n.d.; Staker & Horn, 2012). Here a number of courses are available for students in grades 6-12 to complete online. A primer course is necessary before an online course can be taken, to familiarise students with the technology and requirements for completing the course. The online course can then be completed remotely or using a school cyber-lounge. Quakertown Community School District (n.d.) believe that, along with the general educational outcomes associated with the courses, skills are developed in writing, self-motivation, time management, and goal attainment. Attaining these skills prior to undergraduate education can be beneficial, as undergraduate courses are becoming more and more blended and online (Allen, Seaman, & Garrett, 2007). The A La Carte Model is considered to be a disruptive innovation because, although it is built over a traditional education framework, there is a necessity for new facilities and staff changes in implementing the A La Carte Model.

Individual Rotation Model

The *Individual Rotation Model* is similar to the Station Rotation Model, but with an individual student rotation method instead of a class-level rotation (Staker & Horn, 2012). Students rotate between stations on a fixed schedule according to a customised playlist which may or may not include all available stations. It is considered BL if at least one of these stations is online. This model allows for an individualised pathway for students, although it is more rigid in terms of student progress (Walne, 2012). This fixed scheduling will suit some students, but not others. A successful implementation of the Individual Rotation Model can be seen in grades K-8 at A.L. Holmes Elementary School (Walne, 2012). The model was introduced here in an effort increase educational outcomes in the struggling school. Teachers had to ascend a steep learning curve over a short period to adapt to the new system, but by the fourth month, all of the teachers involved reportedly would not change back to traditional teaching given the opportunity. At A.L. Holmes Elementary School, F2F teachers work closely with onsite Program Managers and online staff to develop and implement individualised learning strategies for their students. Data from the students are closely monitored, assessed, and adjusted if necessary to maximise learning. The Individual Rotation Model is considered to be a disruptive innovation because it requires professional development of teachers, role changes of staff, and the addition of program management staff. In some cases, the Individual Rotation Model has also involved custom-built facilities to enhance the experience (Walne, 2012).

Enriched Virtual Model

The final model described by Staker and Horn (2012) is the *Enriched Virtual Model*. The models so far have included online components in their F2F educational framework. The Enriched Virtual Model is different in that it is better explained by offering F2F components to its online educational framework. That is, it offers F2F components perhaps once or twice a week, maybe less, while the rest is delivered online. The Enriched Virtual Model has similarities with the A La Carte Model, except instead of a select few courses being offered online, the whole school is offered this way. Successful implementation of the Enriched Virtual Model can be seen in grades 8-12 at the Albuquerque eCADEMY (Staker & Horn, 2012). Here students attend an initial F2F meeting, and then if they desire to continue, and are able to maintain a minimum C grade, the remainder of the course can be completed offsite and online. Onsite F2F interaction is available to struggling students and those who request it. This model is regarded as a disruptive innovation, as it is much closer to fully online learning than traditional learning on the BL continuum. Professional teachers would likely make up a much smaller percentage of the staff than in other models, with technical staff and paraprofessionals making up a larger portion.

Models Efficacy

As can be seen from these models, the ratio of F2F to online or other technology use is not black and white. This ratio not only varies between the models, but also within the models. This is further complicated in that research assessing what proportion of technology or online components is most beneficial is limited and often confounded. For example, there are suggestions that the inclusion of online components in BL improves student outcomes up to about a ratio of 50/50 (Bernard et al., 2014), yet other research suggests that low to medium use of technology within the classroom is more beneficial than high use (Schmid et al., 2014). These studies are by no means conclusive, however, and at least two main flaws can be identified in them. Firstly, most BL studies have been short term, and largely very short term. Secondly, students were generally not prepared at all, or had minimal pre-exposure to the technology use; those that were pre-exposed to technology were found to have better academic outcomes than those without (Schmid et al., 2014). Thus, issues with respect to duration and participant training appear to present limitations for much of the existing BL research. Turning to large-scale evaluation of the BL research, a widely cited meta-analysis by Means et al. (2013) showed no significant difference between purely F2F and purely online education. Overall, we suggest that making judgements based on short-term studies with unprepared students is not recommended (a later section will discuss potential ways to prepare students for BL), but our aim is not to criticise the authors of the above-mentioned research. Rather, we seek to point out that much more research is necessary before any strong claims can be made about the specifics of BL, including which blend is best. Until a number of quality, longitudinal studies have been carried out, the debate of what blend is the best is hypothetical at best.

Although perhaps the most comprehensive in descriptions of BL models, the Staker and Horn (2012) models described above should not be seen as the only available options, or even the best available options. Instead, the best option of BL model for a school will be discovered or developed when a number of important questions are answered; questions different for each school. These are questions surrounding curriculum-fit, technology availability, cost-effectiveness, and evidence of learning outcomes (PERC, 2014). Also to be considered are socio-economic factors, geographic factors, school staff quality, and funding availability (Holker et al., 2008). Best practice does not exist in BL; at least not yet (Partridge, Ponting, & McCay, 2011; Watson, 2008). Rather, what the research tells us is that we need to aim for appropriate practice: practice that is adapted to the school staff, students, parents, and community (Holker et al., 2008). This understanding supports our earlier suggestion to maintain a broader, more flexible definition for BL, by compelling us to take a "needs-based" approach to the implementation of BL.

Blended Learning Elements

In order to develop a BL model adapted to a particular school, a more thorough understanding of the elements available for use in BL is necessary. This section will consider dimensions of BL before focussing in on some specific elements and how they relate to the BL dimensions.

Ten overarching dimensions are thought to be important considerations in BL (Vanourek, 2011; Watson et al., 2011). Some of these are less relevant, perhaps, to the current paper, but need to be considered nonetheless. These include *Reach*; will the BL being implemented be available to just the local district, to the state, to the country, or will it be available globally? Also, *School Type* can affect BL implementation, such as public, private, contract, charter schools, as well as who retains *Operational Control*? For example, will a local board, a regional authority, the state, or an independent vendor be charged with operational control? Another dimension to consider is the *Grade Level*. Although the decision of which grades are having BL implemented is perhaps not so relevant to this paper, what elements and the extent of BL being implemented into different grade levels needs to be considered. This will be discussed more below. The above dimensions are important considerations, but are considered less relevant to this paper because they are decisions to be made perhaps by politicians, CEOs, and boards. The current paper is focussed on decisions to be made concerning implementation and running of BL from the ground level. For example, decisions made by the school(s) involved.

Of the ten dimensions of BL (Vanourek, 2011; Watson et al., 2011), the following seven are considerations which will impact on what the BL will look like within the school. *Comprehensiveness* of the BL implementation, whether supplemental BL courses will be

39

added to the school or if all of the school's courses will be transformed, may be informed by why BL is being implemented. For example, some schools will initially begin by providing BL courses for credit recovery or to satisfy advanced students (Michigan Virtual University, n.d.). This may be the intended extent of BL implementation. On the other hand, a major transformation of the school may be intended, to modernise the school or to improve overall student performance. This, of course, requires careful planning and design, not to mention available support and funding.

The *Location* is another dimensional consideration. Will an existing school be adapted to suit BL? Will a new purpose-made facility be built? Will students spend most of their time studying from home? Or will there be a combination of these locations? A related, but different, dimension concerns the *Type of Instruction*; how much of the BL will be F2F and how much will be online? This is somewhat different from location because, for example, online components may take place on campus or remotely.

Two closely related dimensions also requiring consideration are the extent of *Teacher-Student Interaction* and *Student-Student Interaction*. Will the students be largely left to their own devices or have efficient means of communication with the teacher? Will students have little communication with other students, or will there be channels to allow for collaboration between students? Considering type of communications then leads to how the communication will be delivered. *Delivery* can be synchronous or asynchronous. Synchronous delivery is involved in live video conferencing, for example. People can interact in real time. Asynchronous delivery is involved in email or a discussion board, for example. There is a delay between communications. One person will send a message and then wait for a reply. Both forms of delivery have their place, and both may be included in a BL course.

The extent of these dimensions may be influenced by the selection of BL model(s) to be implemented into the school. However, a knowledge of some specific elements which may form the basis of a BL course and how they have been used can shed light on how dimensions may be involved.

Synchronous/Asynchronous Delivery

First, synchronous delivery will be discussed. Online synchronous methods can provide education to those with various geographical restraints (e.g. remote, travelling, expatriates) and special needs (e.g. medical, special education), in a way that is less disjointed than asynchronous methods. Hastie, Hung, Chen, and Kinshuk (2010) have elaborated on how synchronous BL may look and be used in their *Blended Synchronous Learning Model* (BSLM). They describe nine synchronous BL modes, each made up from a combination of cyber classrooms (remote online location, for example students home or on-campus computer lab), physical classrooms, teacher(s), and student(s). The number of cyber classrooms, physical classrooms, teachers, and students can also vary. For example, Mode 1 includes one cyber class, any number of online students, perhaps in residential groups, but also a number of physical classrooms with more students. This mode does not include a teacher, but perhaps a field expert who presents information and is involved in discussion with the students. The field expert may even be in the field at the time of the class, for example, treating an animal at a zoo in another country. This experience would be very costly or impossible in a traditional classroom.

Of course, a synchronous BL element might merely involve one or more teachers presenting content live online to offsite students, such as Mode 2 of the BSLM, or a remote teacher presenting content to students in multiple campus classrooms, such as Mode 4 (Hastie et al., 2010). Synchronous online delivery has been found to be perceived by

41

students as no different to F2F delivery in social presence (Francescato et al., 2006). The same study also found cooperation, collaboration, and satisfaction rating from students to be the same between the two modalities. Synchronous online methods have also been shown to allow for more social interaction between students (O'Dwyer, Carey, & Kleiman, 2007). It is not surprising, then, that synchronous methods (e.g. live video conference) have outperformed asynchronous methods (e.g. discussion boards) in collaborative tasks (Strang, 2013). Synchronous online delivery can also be used to provide training on required technology use, including asynchronous technology use (Hastie et al., 2010). Although this obviously would aid student progress through a course directly, it may also be used to develop the skills of parents (AKA home tutors) in supervising home education. Utilising parents as student supervisors and requiring less real estate on campus, economic benefits may also ensue.

Although there are many benefits to synchronous online delivery, there may also be related issues (Hastie et al., 2010). Students, and perhaps parents, must be self-organised and conform to the scheduled classes. This includes preparing for the class and setting up required technology on time to commence with the lesson. The issue of time can be magnified when there are time zone differences between teachers and students. In fact, time zone differences may make synchronous delivery untenable. There are also potential difficulties in providing technical support for remote participants of synchronous delivery. Synchronous methods can only be used to provide technology support for remote students if the synchronous technology is functioning properly. The teacher will need to develop skills in the use of the technology, but also in providing adequate attention to online students, especially if the delivery mode is mixed. Thus, although synchronous delivery is ideal in certain circumstances, like all BL elements, it is not the answer to all issues pertaining to BL.

We will now turn our attention to asynchronous online delivery. Email is an asynchronous method, however, it is generally used as a line of communication, not an educational tool. Of all the asynchronous online delivery methods used as an educational tool, discussion boards are likely the most prolific. An online discussion board is generally contained within a course website, allowing for open communication between teachers and students, but also students and other students (Blackmon, 2012). A discussion board may be used, thus, for purely social discussion and for announcements. However, research on the benefits of online discussion boards as an educational tool is mounting (Pena-Shaff & Altman, 2015). For example, a number of studies have identified a positive relationship between discussion board use and student outcomes (e.g. Pena-Shaff & Altman, 2015; Shana, 2009). Provision of a discussion board is not enough to promote improved student outcomes however. To encourage critical thinking in discussion board use, the teacher must also facilitate the discussions in a purposeful but infrequent manner, and ensure that the discussions have an emphasised focus (Arend, 2009). That is, unlike synchronous methods, if a discussion board is setup with clear intentions and focussed topics, students have an opportunity to consider what they post. Once the teacher establishes the topic, their input should then be reduced to occasional facilitation and direction; allowing students to draw conclusions and develop arguments on their own. Those who are involved in posts with more critical and deep thinking based on course content have been found to have significantly better learning outcomes (Bliuc, Ellis, Goodyear, & Piggott, 2009). Giving students an understanding of the purpose of the asynchronous discussion, but also of how it will be graded, has also been found to increase critical thinking (Klisc, Mcgill, & Hobbs,

43

2012). This relinquishing of control by teachers, allowing for student focussed and directed learning is a recurring theme in BL we will see again.

Discussion boards can also increase participation in general, but can be especially useful in including more inhibited students in class discussions (Dengler, 2008). Students who are shy may not participate in F2F discussions, even if it means receiving a lower grade. These same shy students, however, have been found to be more comfortable participating in online discussions (Pena-Shaff & Altman, 2015; Yeh & Lahman, 2007)

Although compulsory discussions can increase participation in discussion boards, they are not always correlated with improved student outcomes (Bliuc, Ellis, Goodyear, & Piggott, 2009). Some students were found to post superficial comments on the discussion board to comply with the assessment task. These types of posts were found to be related to lower overall student grades in the course.

Potential issues involved in asynchronous discussion boards have been uncovered. To begin with, lack of body language and vocal tones can lead to miscommunication (Blackmon, 2012; Yeh & Lahman, 2007). Care must be taken to ensure, not only content, but also tone of expressions are conveyed clearly. A post may be misconstrued and deemed offensive, but because the post creator cannot see the offended expression of the reader, the misunderstanding may not be clarified and lead to tension among participants. Maintaining a positive mood is important for maintaining engagement (Yeh & Lahman, 2007). Too many posts from too many participants can also lead students to disengage from the discussion (Cheung, Hew, & Ling Ng, 2008; Yeh & Lahman, 2007). It also takes time to read and respond on discussion boards. Thus, if the group is too large, the amount of time taken becomes magnified. This may be overcome by dividing large classes into smaller discussion groups. Shana (2009) summarises it well in saying discussion boards should be "learner centred, task oriented, non-threatening and a safe space" (p. 225) for students to interact and learn together.

Web 2.0

Web 2.0 tools are another common element of BL. Web 2.0 is web-based technology characterised by the allowance for user input. That is, Web 2.0 is technically no different to standard static websites except that users can add content which can then be viewed by others. Content can be in different mediums, such as text-based (e.g. Twitter), audio-based (e.g. podcasts), photo-based (e.g. Flickr), or video (e.g. YouTube), or a combination of mediums (e.g. Facebook; McLoughlin & Lee, 2010). Although these tools are largely renowned for their recreational capacities, they are being implemented more and more into education. Web 2.0 allows for self-directed learning to take place by doing, not merely passively viewing (Brown & Adler, 2008).

Blogs are similar to discussion boards, but generally require less frequent but more in-depth posts. They are also less interactive. Comments can generally be made below a blog post, but they are often supplementary. Blogs can allow students to reflect on course content in a less formal way than, for example, an essay (Picciano, 2009). They are advantageous in that they are easy to use, they are self-directed, they do not rely on elaborate or expensive systems to function, and they allow students to submit and update in real-time (Lou et al., 2012). Thus, students can reflect on content presented in class, post their blog, reflect on their own blog, and adjust the blog based on their reflection. Another use of blogging in education can find a teacher providing the blog post for students to comment on (Reyna, 2016). Imbedding a video into the blog can also make this more engaging for students. Reyna (2016) found that a good proportion of the comments to videos imbedded in blogs were reflective (38%), collaborative (25%), and interactive (27%).

Twitter is another text-based Web 2.0 tool which has been used in education. Twitter is a social networking tool that allows participants to post short 140-character *Tweets*. This has potential in education to: allow for continued discussion after lectures; allow students to interact with teachers and other student in a non-confronting way; allow for real-time commentary on lectures; make announcements relating to upcoming events and deadlines; allow for ongoing progress reports on assessable tasks (Junco, Elavsky, & Heiberger, 2013). Student outcomes and engagement have been shown to improve with Twitter use under the right conditions (Junco, Elavsky, & Heiberger, 2013). Faculty involvement is an important aspect. Twitter use needs to be compulsory. Most importantly, however, is that the use of Twitter should be based on a theoretically-driven pedagogical model. The well-planned and designed aspect is another recurring theme of this paper. Using Twitter just because you can does not mean it will be beneficial.

A podcast is an audio recording available in compressed format to download. However, the term podcast can also be used to describe a vodcast, which includes audio and video. YouTube is video and audio clip available for viewing online. These Web 2.0 tools will be grouped together because they can often be used in similar ways. Podcasts and YouTube videos of lecture content is probably the most common use of these tools in education. These can be used by students to clarify and review concepts at a convenient time. However, students have been found to access this material more so in the week leading up to an exam or test (Vajoczki, Watt, Marquis, & Holshausen, 2010). In their study, Vajoczki et al. (2010) found that access to podcasts improved student outcomes overall. They also discovered that, despite initial reservations about the use of podcasts in their classes, teachers largely had positive experiences with them. This included markedly less requests for concept clarification post-lectures.

Another use of podcasts is for assessment. In this case, students may be required to record a podcast on class content or a specified topic and upload it for assessment. This is believed to assess deeper learning than a written assignment (Department of Education and Early Childhood Development, 2012). A podcast is akin to an oral presentation for online students (Picciano, 2009).

Web 2.0 can encourage student-driven learning via autonomy and engagement (McLoughlin & Lee, 2010). Although students often have experience with web 2.0 tools, they do not always see their relevance to learning, requiring scaffolding to guide this process. Having a knowledge of how these everyday applications can be used as educational and upskilling tools, aside from benefitting curriculum-based learning, will allow students to adapt to the modern world (Brown & Adler, 2008). With some guidance, teachers are found to generally support the utility of web 2.0 in the classroom (Jimoyiannis, Tsiotakis, Roussinos, & Siorenta, 2013). However, time and infrastructure limitations, as well as curriculum restrictions, have been cited as potential blocks against implementation for some teachers. Teachers not only need an understanding of web 2.0 tools, but also how they can be integrated into good pedagogical methods of learning (McLoughlin & Lee, 2010).

Online Quizzes

Online quizzes have several benefits over in-class paper quizzes. To begin with, they are easily distributed and accessible to students whenever they want and wherever they are. Also, they can be set up to automatically mark the student results. This can save a lot of time for the teacher. These results can then be immediately fed back to the students to allow them to assess their understanding and progress in the course. This information can also be used by the teacher to assess how individual students and the entire class are

47

progressing and whether there are areas that require further clarification. The online quizzes can also be set up to allow for repeated attempts by students, with immediate feedback to further develop their learning.

Online quizzes can be used in a Flipped Classroom model (Hudson et al., 2015). In this case, students are required to review content prior to class, but also complete the online quiz which is due the night before class. This encourages students to review the content so they do not lose marks for not completing the quiz, which, in turn, increases the quality of discussion in the class. This model was shown to not only improve student outcomes (Hudson et al., 2015), but online quizzes have been shown to be enjoyable for students (Dos, 2014). Although a previous meta-analysis showed mixed results concerning the effectiveness of online quizzes on student outcomes (Means et al., 2009), a more recent meta-analysis supports their use (Spanjers et al., 2015).

Digital Games and Virtual Worlds

Digital games and virtual worlds are increasingly being tested as educational tools (Backlund & Hendrix, 2013; Merchant et al., 2014). It is beyond the scope of this paper to go into depth on what these games and virtual worlds consist of (and we note that this information is often not reported), but suffice to say that these technologies can potentially include almost anything imaginable. Games and virtual worlds have been found to positively influence student outcomes (Merchant et al., 2014). Games, however, have been found to be most effective. Games have been included in many subject areas with largely positive results. In K-12, games have been used in geography (positive outcome), history (positive outcome), health (unclear outcome), mathematics (mixed, majority positive outcome), natural science (positive outcome), physics (positive outcome), problem-solving (mixed outcome), and more (Backlund & Hendrix, 2013). Of the games analysed within the

Backlund and Hendrix (2013) meta-analysis, most of the games were developed for the specific course, although some commercial recreational games were included. This indicates that well designed and relevant digital games can have a positive effect on student outcomes and engagement. Barriers to the use of games as educational tools have also been reported however. These include scepticism by both teachers and students concerning the educational value of the games, time constraints for training teachers, and technological shortcomings of the school or school system.

Virtual worlds are digital environments which can take the form of anything one can imagine. Generally, they involve the use of avatars (digital representations of the user), which are used to interact with this virtual environment. Hew and Cheung (2010), in their review of the virtual world literature, found that they were generally used for three main purposes: for communication; for simulation; and for experiencing. One of the more well-known virtual world applications is Second Life. Second Life is a 3D virtual environment which is played online. Players create an avatar and take part in this virtual world by purchasing or creating objects for their avatar; from clothes to houses. Second Life is available for recreational purposes, but it has also been tested as an educational tool (e.g. Inman, Wright, & Hartman, 2010). In their study, Inman, Wright, and Hartman (2010) found that Second Life can facilitate distance education, role-playing, collaboration and communication, and learning about design. In their suggested steps to implementation of Second Life (which will be elaborated on in a later section), they identify the importance of identifying course objectives and how Second Life might suit these objectives. Once again, the use of Second Life will not work in all circumstances. It may, however, be a beneficial addition to the right course. Second Life was found to have similar barriers to digital games: scepticism about use as an educational tool from students; technical issues; and training required by teachers and students (Inman, Wright, & Hartman, 2010). Additionally, the potential for Second Life to distract students, despite educational intentions, and the potential for exposure to inappropriate content were included as concerns.

Automated Guidance

Automated guidance tools assess and guide individual students through online curricula. An example of this is an intelligent tutoring system, which requires a student to work through a problem using the computer. The computer may give immediate feedback to the student when a step is performed incorrectly, or once the result is submitted. The feedback is in the form of a hint, not explicitly revealing the correct strategy. VanLehn (2011) found that intelligent tutoring systems are nearly as effective as a human tutor in STEM (Science, Technology, Engineering, and Mathematics) subjects. A meta-analysis by Gerard, Matuk, McElhaney, and Linn (2015) found that inclusion of automated guidance led to better learning outcomes than traditional instruction in K-12 when students had low or medium prior content knowledge. Those with high prior knowledge, however, benefitted more from traditional instruction. This was thought to be due to high prior knowledge students' perceptions of the automated guidance being extraneous or moving too slow. Also, high prior knowledge students rarely used hints and available help in the automated guidance tools, despite incorrect responses. This indicates that scepticism of the tool may reduce its effectiveness. Automated guidance tools have been shown to be effective, for example, in science (Leelawong & Biswas, 2008), Language Arts (Wade-stein & Kintsch, 2004), and mathematics (Koedinger & Aleven, 2007). In line with the current paper's topic, automated guidance tools are not intended to replace teachers, but to be supplemental to F2F teaching (VanLehn, 2011).

Learning Management System

A Learning Management System (LMS), otherwise known as Course Management System or Virtual Learning Environment, may be used as the core technology of BL (iNACOL, 2015). It is a system framework which, among other things, allows access to course content and allows communication between relevant parties. Course content may be discussion boards, web 2.0 tools, or any number of online educational tools. Announcements can be made to students within a course or across the school. Individual learning paths can be developed and adjusted for students. Student usage can be logged and student progress can be tracked. The collection, analysis, and representation of student data is in itself an emerging field known as *Learning Analytics* (Gros, 2016). Access to these and other data from the LMS can be allowed or denied to teachers, students, or even parents; allowing parental access to this information can be very useful in K-12, especially if the parent is also the home tutor.

Whether or not to include a LMS when implementing BL into a school, and choosing from the many available options requires assessment of school and course objectives, and research about the different LMS capabilities. It should be made clear that a LMS is not essential when implementing BL; other options are available to allow for organising and accessing of online content. Before considering if and what LMS to use, many considerations need to be addressed. For example, the school objectives, the intended proportion of online content, and the education design and strategies involved. Clearly identifying the intentions for implementing BL will then allow for an informed decision on if an LMS should be incorporated and what LMS would be suitable.

If the decision has been made to incorporate a LMS into the BL design, further questions need to be considered (iNACOL, 2015; Michigan Virtual University, n.d.). Should you choose an existing LMS, either through licensing or open source? Or should you develop your own? Or perhaps you will be better off with a mix of both? The answer to these question will depend on available expertise, resources available (including time), funding available (start-up and ongoing costs), and necessity for customisation. There are pros and cons to licensing a LMS, using an open source LMS, and mixing the two (Michigan Virtual University, n.d.).

Licensing a LMS is beneficial in that it is ready to implement, and support is often provided to setup and maintain the system. On the other hand, licensing a LMS may not allow for customisation, all content must be assessed for quality and curriculum relevance, it does not develop with school, and all upfront and ongoing costs need to be understood.

An open source LMS is free to use, but there is little or no support, and they may be used at the risk of the user. On the positive side, some open source LMSs are customisable and can serve as a starting point for further development. The price is potentially the most attractive aspect to an open source LMS.

If time, funding, and expertise is available, developing a LMS may be the best option. Creating a customised LMS is beneficial in that there is complete control over content, the initial and ongoing development is fully customised to suit the school, the rights to the LMS a fully retained, and to top it off, the product potentially saleable once it is refined. Of course, as eluded to, this requires technical knowhow and large scale projects require temporal and financial resources. Also, smaller schools may struggle to compete with larger schools and companies.

The final option is to mix it up. Different elements may be purchased and others may be created for different courses or even within courses. The extent of purchased software use might even decrease as staff expertise increases.

Examples of other systems available as an add-on to a LMS include a Learning Content Management System (LCMS) and a Student Information System (SIS). A LCMS allows content to be stored in digital repositories which allow for access across courses within the LMS. This is useful in that updates will be applied in the LCMS, which then is supplied to all courses which utilise the content. Meta-data can also be associated with content in the LCMS, which allows for efficient searching for content relevant to a topic. The LCMS is sometimes added to the LMS at a later date, although these need be able to be integrated to function properly.

A SIS stores student demographics, schedules, and performance data. The SIS should integrate with the LMS and allow for student progress outputs. This may be done manually, in an automated fashion, or in real time. A real time SIS will automatically be updated across systems.

Emerging Technologies

There are a number of technologies which are still evolving and being developed which will likely make their way into the BL classroom. Gros (2016) identifies a number of these. Mobile technologies are portable devices which maintain an internet connection. Using the term *M-learning*, research is already being performed to assess how this technology can be used in education (e.g. Park, 2011). Related to this, *Hybridisation* is another technological development which is emerging as a potential educational tool (Gros, 2016). Examples of hybridisation include wearable devices, the internet of things, and augmented reality. These all have the potential to be used as educational tools. For example, augmented reality could allow students to view non-existent objects through their mobile device camera (e.g. smart phone), making it seem as though it were right in front of them. This could be especially beneficial when learning about abstract constructs in mathematics or science (Bujak et al., 2013).

This is not intended to be an all-inclusive description of the elements available for use in a BL model. Instead it is intended to give an overview of some of the more commonly used and emerging elements, and to highlight some pros and cons of each. Hopefully it is glaringly obvious that all of these elements will not be suitable for all subjects, for all grade levels, or for all schools. The ten dimensions important to BL described initially in this section (Vanourek, 2011; Watson et al., 2011) will go some way in identifying appropriate candidates from the elements available to BL. However, we continue to stress that a well-planned and designed BL model, theoretically-driven, and based on course objectives, is the most important aspect of BL implementation.

Student Outcomes

When BL is being discussed, there is generally a lot of talk about perceptions of teachers and students, economic concerns, definitions of this, and models of that... One thing, however, should be of paramount importance to this discussion: *Student Outcomes*. Improving student outcomes is, or at least should be, the driving force behind all educational facilities. In light of this consideration, the following section will review literature which has assessed the effects of BL on student outcomes. Where possible, research will relate directly to grades K-12. However, because quality empirical K-12 research on BL is in short supply (cf. Means, Toyama, Murphy, & Baki, 2013; Spanjers et al., 2015), research from tertiary education will also be included to fill in the gaps, which will be tentatively and very cautiously generalised to K-12.

Student outcomes have largely been positively affected, or at least not detrimentally affected, by BL implementation into grades K-12 (Chandra & Lloyd, 2008; Department of Education and Early Childhood Development, 2012; Liu & Cavanaugh, 2011; Lueken & Ritter, 2015; Means et al., 2009; Tamim et al., 2011). Amidst the literature, there are hints of what has worked and what has not. Of course, as mentioned above, we cannot claim that one aspect is an example of best practice when designing and implementing BL, but we do assert that a tentative outline for appropriate practice may be established from the extant limited literature.

To begin with, students will not always dive into BL without hesitation. If a student is new to BL or online learning, they will probably come into it with an expectation of what K-12 education is *supposed* to be like. This expectation might be something like: the teacher presents content in a traditional classroom where the students face the front of the room; there may or may not be discussion among the group; based on that content there will be assessments, such as tests, written assignments, and other such activities. This is an oversimplification of traditional teaching, but give or take a few innovations, there is usually nothing extravagantly different among traditional classrooms. Now, imagine going through your school life for a number of years, becoming accustomed to what is expected of you, and then suddenly being thrown into a BL experience. That might entail any multitude of new experiences, such as studying content online from home before coming to class where the teacher expects you to have an understanding of the material and be able to be involved in a group discussion about it (Staker & Horn, 2012), being given an assignment to create a video on a topic and upload it to the course website (Department of Education and Early Childhood Development, 2012), or perhaps being asked to go to a computer lab and play a computer game (Inman, Wright, & Hartman, 2010). The importance of these activities for

BL is that, although K-12 students of today are likely to be familiar with the tools being used in these examples, their use in relation to classroom learning may be a source of confusion (Inman, Wright, & Hartman, 2010). It is not surprising, then, that when BL is implemented into the classroom student grades can dip a bit (Lueken & Ritter, 2015). Thus, if a school was to base a decision on whether to implement BL for the first few months or even the first year in light of student outcomes, many schools might decide against it. However, once students become accustomed to what is expected in BL, (and most teachers also need to become accustomed) grades tend to normalise or even exceed original levels (Lueken & Ritter, 2015). This should not preclude any adjustment or refinement in these early stages, but it is important to understand and consider this for the initial decisions that need to be made.

The process of student familiarisation with BL may be hastened with some focussed training. For example, training might be initially provided for students to familiarise them with the online educational tools (Junco, Elavsky, & Heiberger, 2013; Lim, Kim, Chen, & Ryder, 2008). Even if the students are familiar with the tools in a recreational sense, adjustments in use may be necessary to suit its educational purposes (Hudson et al., 2015). Knowing how to use the BL elements is one thing, but knowing why they are being used is also important. Transparency as to why students are using online educational tools seems to be an important aspect of their acceptance and engagement with them. This, in turn, has been found to positively impact on their learning (Junco, Elavsky, & Heiberger, 2013; Lim et al., 2008; Reyna, 2016). As previously mentioned, BL literature has many examples where teachers relinquish control over their students. Transparency in rationale for using a teaching method is one such example. This allows students to have a greater sense of their learning journey.

Besides having an awareness of their learning journey, BL can also allow students to have more control over it. In a traditional F2F classroom, if a student loses track of the discussion or does not understand a major concept being addressed, the remainder of the lesson can be confusing and may even make the student feel inadequate. The availability of online content or self-paced computer-based content can allow a student to take time to grasp difficult concepts, to repeat content that has not quite sunk in; to progress at a pace suitable to them (Department of Education and Early Childhood Development, 2012). The research is somewhat mixed in terms of results and findings concerning BL and self-pacing, and allowance of extra time for students has been cited as a potential confound in the BL research of Means et al. (2013). Is the affordance of extra time really a confounding variable though? Is extra time affordance not an offering that BL can make above and beyond the traditional classroom? We also note that students from a background of speaking a different language can especially benefit from being able to slow classes to a more comfortable pace (Chandra & Lloyd, 2008). At the same time, and potentially in the same computer lab, more advanced students may be progressing at a faster rate, not having to wait for the rest of the class to catch up. The issue of pace, therefore, appears to offer more positive effects than negative in terms of student engagement.

The personalisation afforded by BL does not stop with the pace in the classroom; it can extend to conforming to individual learning styles. Because a course is no longer bound by a single stream - the pace and content directed by the teacher – students can engage with different resources to a greater or lesser extent, and develop a learning path suited to their learning style (Department of Education and Early Childhood Development, 2012; DiPietro, Ferdig, Black, & Preston, 2008). This may be achieved by providing options for students to choose how they wish to learn or by identifying student learning styles and providing suitable personalised content, with the former requiring more effort from the student and the latter requiring more effort from the teacher.

Although the personalisation and independence afforded to students in BL is often seen as a positive, it is only positive if the student is capable of dealing with it (Vaughan, 2007). Some have suggested that, in order for students to get the most out of BL, students need to develop self-regulated learning skills (Azevedo & Cromley, 2004; Bernard et al., 2014; Chang, 2005). Zimmerman (2000) describes a three phase model of self-regulated learning (Dabbagh & Kitsantas, 2011). First a student must plan and set goals in the *fore-thought phase*. These are based on pre-existing beliefs and interests related to the required learning task. The *performance phase* then finds the student initiating the plans made in the fore-thought phase in order to reach the desired goals. This includes using learning strategies and monitoring progress. The *self-reflection phase* then allows the student to evaluate their learning path and strategies in relation to goal attainment. This phase may lead to adjustment in the fore-thought, where the cycle begins again. This self-regulated learning can be trained in students through, for example, the use of journals, reflection tasks, and time management tasks (Zimmerman et al., 1996; Chang, 2005). In fact, improved student achievement has been linked with self-regulated learning training sessions as short as 30 minutes (Azevedo & Cromley, 2004). Incorporating the building of self-regulated learning into BL courses or school curriculum can not only improve grades, but also student satisfaction (Puzziferro, 2008), potentially decreasing issues of withdrawal rates (Florida TaxWatch, 2007). This would then allow for increased independent, self-directed learning over a student's K-12 education, potentially allowing for increased OL and decreased F2F blends, but would also be preparatory for tertiary education.

Relinquishing some control over student learning may seem like an empowering exercise for students, but the teacher still needs to be able to efficiently and effectively monitor the performance of the class and its individual students (Parkes, Zaka, & Davis, 2011). Keeping track of the progress of individuals within a large class can be challenging when using traditional methods. This may lead to struggling students falling behind and more advanced students becoming bored. Efficient progress evaluation is something BL can offer. Frequent online quizzes, for example, can allow a teacher to assess whether the class requires further guidance in certain domains, and whether individual students are lagging behind. Perhaps best of all, this can be automated. Once the quizzes are setup online, they can be made available automatically at a certain time, the student scores can be automatically calculated, and results can be displayed in an easy-to-read format. At a glance, teachers are able to see how the entire class is performing overall, but also whether there are certain students who require further assistance. Furthermore, this function is just as easy with large classes as with small groups. Similar functions are also available for automated guidance software. In fact, even parents could potentially have access to real-time data of their child's learning progress.

Another method for assessing student progress is in their behavioural engagement data. For example, if a BL course requires students to access the LMS several times a week or for certain lengths of time, this information may be made available to the teacher. A teacher will be able to notice if a student has not been accessing the LMS and approach the student regarding this issue (Liu & Cavanaugh, 2011). Keeping track of online content engagement can give teachers early warning sign of struggling students. This may seem like an arbitrary measure of student progress, but time spent on the LMS has been found to correlate with better grades (Liu & Cavanaugh, 2011).

Student engagement itself has been found to increase with well-designed BL courses, in turn, improving student outcomes (Bernard et al., 2014; Department of Education and Early Childhood Development, 2012; Dos, 2014; Kim, Park, Cozart, & Lee, 2015; Lim, Kim, Chen, & Ryder, 2008; McNaught, Lam, & Cheng, 2012). BL can affect students differently (Chandra & Lloyd, 2008; Liu & Cavanaugh, 2011). Some students have been found to prefer lecture-style learning; believing that online content should be supplemental (Chandra & Lloyd, 2008). This, however, is not the norm, and perhaps due to a student technological ability or course BL design (Department of Education and Early Childhood Development, 2012; Dos, 2014; Lim, Kim, Chen, & Ryder, 2008; Lim, Morris, & Kupritz, 2007; McNaught, Lam, & Cheng, 2012; Mentzer, Cryan, & Teclehaimanot, 2007; Spanjers et al., 2015). Students have been shown to find BL to be engaging for a number of reasons (Department of Education and Early Childhood Development, 2012). For example, students may enjoy the flexibility in time and location (Chandra & Lloyd, 2008). Students in K-12, being younger, may enjoy the experience of rotating between learning station of different modalities (Staker & Horn, 2012). It is not hard to understand that this would be seen by younger students as more engaging than a traditional lecture-style class; sitting for long periods while listening to an adult speak is not generally a young child's idea of fun. Also, as mentioned above, developing your own learning path and setting a suitable pace has also found to be more engaging (Department of Education and Early Childhood Development, 2012). Of course, having access to field experts or environments via video conferencing, not possible without BL, can also engage students. With such potential to engage students with interactive, student-focussed, self-directed content, if teachers are finding that students are not engaging in the learning process, it is likely the design of the BL model being used that is at fault.

A major factor which can affect student engagement (Borup, Graham, & Davies, 2012; Shea & Bidjerano, 2010; Kim, Park, Cozart, & Lee, 2015), achievement (Bernard et al., 2014; Bernard et al., 2009), and retention (Welch, 2012) in BL is social interaction. Social interaction between students and the teacher is obviously important (Bernard et al., 2009; DiPietro, Ferdig, Black, & Preston, 2008; Moore & Kearsley, 2005; Holmberg, 2003), but so too is interactions between the students themselves (Bernard et al., 2009; DiPietro et al., 2008; Salomon, 2000). It is perhaps the social aspect which leads to improved student outcomes in BL compared to purely online education (Means et al., 2009). Bernard et al. (2014) suggest that the more technologies that promote interactions between teachers and students, and between student and other students the more improved student outcomes will be. These social interactions can have cognitive, emotional, and motivational benefits on students (Holmberg, 2003; Kanuka & Anderson, 1999; Moore & Kearsley, 2005; Salomon, 2000). Thus, not only does socialisation improve student satisfaction and personal development, it also can improve academic achievement.

Implementing BL into a course or school is not without potential issues from the student's point of view. Besides those issues already described, BL has been deemed to be more demanding by some students, misperceptions of less work requirements in BL can lead to student difficulties, grades have been found to suffer with incomplete assessments due to poor time management, the initial transition to BL can be difficult to deal with, and self-efficacy, whether real or perceived, can lead to disengagement in students (Mentzer, Cryan, & Teclehaimanot, 2007; Parkes, Zaka, & Davis, 2011; Poon, 2013; Spanjers et al., 2015; Vaughan, 2007). A history of being a passive learner does not prepare students for undertaking BL. Upskilling in necessary areas, such as technology-use and self-regulated learning, can improve student achievement before they are fully immersed in BL.

Alternatively, an incremental transition from more F2F components to more OL components would benefit students in a whole school BL implementation. Each of the student issues described here can be overcome with preparation and good design.

Besides the intended curriculum-based learning objectives that are strived for in educational facilities, BL has been found to lead to some perhaps unintended learning outcomes. To begin with, there is the contemporary literacy and skills concerning digital technology (Department of Education and Early Childhood Development, 2012; Parkes, Zaka, & Davis, 2011). Computers and the internet are becoming more and more prevalent in our day to day lives, not to mention in our working lives. Thus, having experience and confidence with digital technology, beyond their recreational use, can only benefit graduating students. This is apparent when reviewing the literature on student outcomes from BL at a tertiary level. For example, perceived ease of use of e-learning tools, perceived usefulness of e-learning tools, and ability to work independently were found to predict course final grade in tertiary education (Arbaugh, 2014; Galy, Downey, & Johnson, 2011). Students involvement in their own learning process has also been shown to allow teachers and students to develop a mutual understanding and trust (Department of Education and Early Childhood Development, 2012). Positive interactions with the instructor have also been found to improve learning outcomes at a tertiary level (Arbaugh, 2014). Student resourcefulness, higher-order thinking, and deeper understanding of their learning style have also been shown to improve in a well-designed BL course (Department of Education and Early Childhood Development, 2012; Parkes, Zaka, & Davis, 2011). Taken together, beyond the K-12 curriculum, students in well-designed BL will be more prepared for tertiary education and beyond.

One thing should be made very clear here: not only should a great deal of caution be taken when generalising tertiary level BL research to K-12, but research in K-12 should also be read with caution. This is for two reasons: (1) the small number of K-12 studies cannot provide strong support their findings. Until studies have been replicated and the specific features that are having an effect are identified, existing findings are only tentative, even if the research design is of a high quality; (2) Because a certain BL element or model has worked for a particular school or schools, it does not mean it will work for every school. Differences in many factors, such as community culture, sociodemographic make-up of students, funding availability, and political climate, to name just a few, may impact on the success of any form of BL implementation. This should not scare off any potential BL implementation, but should forewarn of the necessity to continuously plan, design, evaluate, and adjust.

Teacher Professional Development

Teachers are required to master content, pedagogy, and now with BL, technology (Koehler, Mishra, & Cain, 2013). Hopefully existing teachers are already well-versed in content and pedagogy, leaving just the technology...or *is* this the case? This section will review research surrounding teacher professional development (PD) in relation to BL. We note, however, that there is room for improvement in the literature for this area (Barbour, 2012; Harms et al., 2006; Torrisi-Steele & Drew, 2013). Indeed, the need for more research seems to be a recurring theme in BL, but teacher PD does have a strong theoretical basis outside of BL.

What better way to train teachers in the planning and design of BL than with BL. In fact, Hastie et al. (2010) have devoted Mode five of their Blended Synchronous Learning

Model to teacher professional development. This makes sense for a number of reasons. Firstly, teachers can be involved remotely. This allows teachers to upskill in between school semesters, even if they are out of the area (although be aware of time zone differences; Hastie et al., 2010). Secondly, a professional, external to the school, knowledgeable in the ways of BL, can be employed to train up teachers. This can be especially beneficial in the initial stages of BL implementation when the whole of school staff may be naïve to BL (Hastie et al., 2010; Weiß & Bader, 2010). Once the school is confident and competent in BL, professional development can happen internally. Thirdly, if BL has been piloted at the school, teachers-in-training may be able to remotely view actual BL classes taking place; informative in itself. Besides the synchronous methods for upskilling teachers, a number of other BL strategies may be used. For example, Weiß and Bader (2010) propose a training model where teachers have an initial F2F session to introduce technologies, build confidence, and overcome technical difficulties. An online phase then finds the teachers completing modules independently over 3 or 4 weeks. The training is then rounded off with another F2F session where the teachers actually use the technology as they would in a classroom environment. Teachers should also be provided with a forum where they can discuss issues and support one another through the process. If it is known what technology will be used by the teachers-in-development, the same technology should be used in their professional development (Davis & Rose, n.d.). Studies suggest that the experience of using the technology, alone, will help develop the teachers and increase their use of technology in the classroom (Weiß & Bader, 2010). Outcomes of the training should be assessed, for example, with the use of pre- and post-training surveys measuring attitudes towards and confidence in technology use. The collection of data concerning PD is imperative to a successful overall training program, and feedback on the training should also be sought. A non-participant control group would ideally be included as a comparison group for research purposes, although this may not be as important for individual implementation situations.

As eluded to in the introduction of this section, just increasing knowledge on the use of technology available for BL is not enough to design a successful BL course. A teacher needs to master content, pedagogy, and technology, but also to understand how these elements interact in various ways and, in particular, how to design scenarios that integrate pedagogy and technology appropriately within a given discipline (Class & Schneider, 2014). This is the basis for TPACK (Technological Pedagogical And Content Knowledge; Koehler, Mishra, & Cain, 2013), a framework for upskilling teachers in BL techniques. TPACK builds on the work of Shulman (1986), which described a necessity for teachers to have Content Knowledge (knowledge of the subject being taught), Pedagogical Knowledge (knowledge of how developmental, social, and cognitive theories can manifest to produce desirable learning outcomes in the classroom), but also Pedagogical Content Knowledge (necessary for a teacher to "interpret...the subject matter, find...multiple ways to represent it, and adapt...the instructional materials to alternative conceptions and students' prior knowledge"; Koehler, Mishra, & Cain, 2013, p. 15). TPACK expands on this idea by asserting that Technological Knowledge (a fluid state of maintaining knowledge of technology, requiring ongoing development to be mindful of how technology can be used to reach set goals) should also be included when teaching using BL. This, then, leads to another set of amalgamations of knowledge types. These are:

- Technological Content Knowledge: Being aware that certain content and technologies will pair together suitably, and others will not.
- Technological Pedagogical Knowledge: Technologies are not always created specifically for education. However, with Technological Pedagogical Knowledge, a

teacher will understand how and where it will produce the best learning outcomes for students.

- Technological Pedagogical Content Knowledge: This is an amalgamation of the above knowledge types. Known as TPACK, this is what is thought to be required to design and implement BL in an efficient and effective way in order to promote engaged students with good student outcomes.

When TPACK is developed, a teacher is able to incorporate technology into a course, not as an add-on, but as a beneficial ingredient in the BL experience (Koehler, Mishra, & Cain, 2013). Issues, however, surround how to develop and to measure TPACK. This is made especially difficult with the fluidity of TK. Measurement of TPACK may be possible within an institution if availability of technologies is limited to current products. Each advancement in technology, however, would require further development of teachers' Technical Knowledge, and the amalgamation knowledges that follow.

Regardless of this theoretical knowledge framework, there are examples where teachers or groups of teachers have successfully designed and implemented BL that have improved student outcomes in K-12 (e.g. Department of Education and Early Childhood Development, 2012; Heafner & Friedman, 2008; Lueken & Ritter, 2015; Pereira et al., 2007; Ümit Yapici & Akbayin, 2012) and at a tertiary level (e.g. Baig, 2015; Lim et al., 2008; Spanjers et al., 2015). Research that has found no difference between BL and traditional teaching, however, seems to lack finesse in their design (e.g. Dell, Low, & Wilker, 2010; Lim, Morris, & Kupritz, 2007; Roscoe, 2012; York, 2008). This goes back to the notion that it is not that BL is better or worse than traditional teaching, but the course design that influences success (Dell, Low, & Wilker, 2010; Roscoe, 2012). Well-designed BL will trump a poorly designed traditional course; well-designed traditional teaching will trump a poorly designed BL course. BL, however, is not limited to traditional teaching tools, which in itself is advantageous.

Much of the literature on teacher professional development in online learning is anecdotal and lacks details (Barbour, 2012; Dede, 2009; Harms et al., 2006). Although professional development program evaluation research is not abundant in relation to BL, there is a set of competencies and standards emerging from research in BL. Some of these have been assembled to aid evaluation of teachers and courses (e.g. iNACOL, 2011; Powell, Rabbitt, & Kennedy, 2014). The International Association for K-12 Online Learning (iNACOL; 2011) have developed National Standards for Quality Online Teaching. Available for download, this list of standards allows for the assessment of teacher capabilities in teaching BL. For example, they believe a teacher should know "the primary concepts and structures of effective online instruction and [be] able to create learning experiences to enable student success" (p. 4) and that the "online teacher understands and is able to use a range of technologies, both existing and emerging, that effectively support student learning and engagement in the online environment" (p. 5). If a program of professional development for teachers beginning BL is not available, developing such a program that conforms to these standards might be a good starting point. As can be seen, however, there is little guidance on how to actually develop these skills.

Powell, Rabbitt, and Kennedy (2014) have assembled the *Blended Learning Teacher Competency Framework*. This lists mindsets, qualities, adaptive skills, and technical skills that a BL teacher should endeavour to develop. Examples of the competencies are "Shift from teacher-led instruction to student-centred learning for the purposes of meeting individual needs and fostering engagement and motivation" (p. 10) and "Create learning environments that are flexible and personalized, dependent on real-time data, direct

67

observation, and interaction with and feedback from students" (p. 10). Once again, these competencies have some great ideas and direction for BL teachers, but they often lack specifics.

Teacher professional development will require time (Michigan Virtual University, n.d.). Depending on what BL elements are being incorporated into a course and the extent of the BL implementation into the school, not all competencies may be required, at least at the initial stages of implementation. These competencies fall into four broad categories: technical skills; educational skills; communication skills; and ethical knowledge.

First of these to be addressed is *Technical Skills*. As well as being able to efficiently and effectively use existing technology, teachers should maintain an up-to-date understanding of relevant emerging technologies (iNACOL, 2011; Powell, Rabbitt, & Kennedy, 2014). Social media, for example, is used frequently in a teacher's private life (being comparative to the general public) and in some aspects of professional life, but this does not necessarily translate to classroom use (Seaman & Tinti-kane, 2013). Although recreational use of technology by teachers is common, a teacher's belief that students may be more competent with the technology than themselves can reduce a teacher's inclination to implement it into the classroom (Weiß & Bader, 2010). Instead they opt for techniques which favours their own skill sets over the students'. With this in mind, it is not surprising that teachers with an interest in emerging technologies have been found to be more successful in BL (DiPietro, Ferdig, Black, & Preston, 2008). The move from recreational use to educationally proficient use of technology requires training (Reyna, 2016), both general and discipline-focused (Davis, & Rose, n.d.; Michigan Virtual University, n.d.).

Along with the specific educational tools used in the classroom, teachers should be able to organise and manage the online learning environment using LMS or another online system (Michigan Virtual University, n.d.; Powell, Rabbitt, & Kennedy, 2014). Teachers should be confident in using automated online grading technology (Michigan Virtual University, n.d.). Automation in grading and assessing can make the process much more efficient. Once these grades and other information are fed into the computer, teachers than should be able to access and understand the student data (iNACOL, 2011; Powell, Rabbitt, & Kennedy, 2014). An understanding of student data should then inform what happens in the classroom.

The second broad competency that will be discussed is *Education Skills*. Although it is expected that a teacher will already be well-practiced in skills relating to education, BL lends itself to some variations from the traditional classroom. To begin with, learning objectives need to adjusted and adapted between F2F and online components (Mortera-Gutierrez, 2006). F2F instruction tends to be more teacher-focussed. Online components, however, require more of a student-focus, as teachers may not be present to guide students through online components. Thus, students must be encouraged to develop independence and self-direction in their learning (Azevedo & Cromley, 2004; Bernard et al., 2014; Chang, 2005; Michigan Virtual University, n.d.; Powell, Rabbitt, & Kennedy, 2014). To aid students' active learning, teachers need to be able to understand how technology can effectively engage students while enhancing their learning (Davis, & Rose, n.d.; iNACOL, 2011; Lowes, 2005). Teachers must also clearly define assessment pieces and indicate expected learning outcomes; transparency in rationale for performing a task can help guide student learning paths (Mortera-Gutierrez, 2006; Reyna, 2016). BL design should be clear and simple to understand by the students (Kistow, 2011; Parkes, Zaka, & Davis, 2011; Weiss, 2014). Of course, students may also require initial training in the use of technologies, especially to direct them towards more of an educational focus (Reyna, 2016).

Obviously teachers should not just place students in front of computer and let them teach themselves. Teachers must guide students through content and adapt content to the student (Michigan Virtual University, n.d.). How is this done? To begin with, teachers must create and implement valid and reliable assessment instruments and procedures (iNACOL, 2011). With frequent and regular assessment tasks, teachers can use real-time student data to adjust content to improve learning outcomes. Data should be used to assess student strengths and weaknesses to create a flexible, personalised learning experience (DiPietro et al., 2008; Powell, Rabbitt, & Kennedy, 2014). Along with student data, teachers should make assessments of student progress based on student feedback, observation, and qualitative interactions. Student data can also be available to the student (and student parents) to promote ownership of learning. This can help to motivate a student and allow them to self-assess; a beneficial skill in itself.

The next competency to be addressed is *Communication Skills*. Communication skills in BL need to also incorporate technical skills. For example, teachers need to able to communicate effectively through digital channels (Michigan Virtual University, n.d.; Mortera-Gutierrez, 2006). This goes beyond sending emails (although that is important to know). BL teachers will be required to understand, among other things, how to make online announcements, to give students access to online content and inform them of the necessary tasks to complete, to interact with student parents, provide them with student data output, and be able to describe what it means. Communication skills are also necessary in the classroom. Beyond the general communication which takes place between students in a F2F context, BL teachers need to communicate with students online with prompt and frequent feedback so students maintain engagement (Davis, & Rose, n.d.; DiPietro et al., 2008; iNACOL, 2011; Mortera-Gutierrez, 2006), with clear indication of expected learning outcomes (Mortera-Gutierrez, 2006), with transparency and explicit rationale for technology use (Reyna, 2016), and to proactively encourage feedback to allow for personalised learning (DiPietro et al., 2008; Powell, Rabbitt, & Kennedy, 2014). Communication skills are important in all forms of education. The above provides some indication of communication skill development required in BL.

The last broad competency to be addressed is *Ethical Knowledge*. Ethical knowledge relating to BL is not too far removed from traditional education. A teacher needs to understand, model, and encourage ethical, legal, and safe behaviour, whether online or F2F (iNACOL, 2011). This not only includes understanding how the students should behave and how teachers should behave around students, but teachers also need to be aware of copyright law. This paper will not expand on this, as laws and policy vary between countries, states, and schools. It is, however, important to be aware that professional development needs to address these concerns.

Although perhaps quite general and broad, hopefully a picture of the potential of BL is forming. BL should not merely swap F2F lectures with online video, or just incorporate a discussion board for a digital communication channel. BL, if it is to be successful, requires well-planned and designed strategies to engage students and allow them to develop ownership and independence in their learning journey. Time to develop these competencies and incremental BL implementation can alleviate the burden on teachers in their professional development towards BL.

Implementing Blended Learning

Methods of implementing BL into a school will depend on many factors. There is much to consider prior to implementation. Of course, starting points of schools will also vary. Although every schools journey to implement BL will be different, there are some considerations that will need to be made in every case, and some that will only be relevant to some schools. This section will provide some guidance, based on the literature, of what the process may look like.

It is assumed, in this section, that the implementation of BL will be performed on an existing school. This may not always be the case. A school may not have previously existed, in which case a BL school will be developed to a set of objectives, not implemented as such. Although much of the following will still be relevant to such a case, some of the language may not quite align.

There are many reasons a school may choose to implement BL. For example, it may be to increase student numbers, to improve student outcomes, to provide flexible options to students, to increase prestige, or to take advantage of the efficiency of computers (Cavanaugh et al., 2004; Horn & Staker, 2011; Sharpe, Benfield, Roberts, & Francis, 2006). The reason for implementing BL into a school may also influence the extent of BL implementation. For example, a school may just want to provide a means to support struggling students or advanced students (Cavanaugh et al., 2004; Watson, 2008). In this case, the rest of the school may continue as normal. A school might tentatively pilot a BL course to assess how it affects student engagement and learning (Department of Education and Early Childhood Development, 2012). This may be the first step towards whole-school implementation. On the other hand, a school might have strong established intentions to become the school of choice when it comes to BL and plan for a complete overhaul of the existing system (Staker & Horn, 2012). Each of these options is possible, depending on time, budget, policy, and culture.

The readiness of a school to implement BL can decide what extent of implementation will take place. Abas, Kaur, and Harun (2005) outlined how *eLearning readiness* might look. They describe eight levels of eLearning readiness, which should transfer nicely to BL: (1) *Environmental Readiness* – the society needs to be accepting of BL (this may be seen in policies and may require promotional strategies to change); (2) *Cultural readiness* – the school culture needs to be accepting of BL; (3) *Management readiness* – support for BL needs to be provided by the institution; (4) *Personnel readiness* – not only do teachers need to be prepared and supportive of BL, but technical staff may need to be recruited to implement and maintain the new technologies; (5) *Learner readiness* – students need to be prepared and supported, especially in the initial stages of the transition to BL; (6) *Financial readiness* – the costs necessary to implementation of BL will vary on its extent, but there will be initial spending and ongoing cost of BL which will need to be provided; (7) *Technical readiness* – the technological infrastructure of the school needs to be able to support the BL implementation; (8) *Content readiness* – educational content then needs to be licensed for use or developed. Once these eight levels of readiness are satisfied, the transition to BL *should* run smoothly. Of course some of these will require a lot more work than others, depending on their current status and the extent of implementation. We will now discuss some of the specifics and obstacles that may be involved in the process.

Lack of staff backing has been found to be an obstacle to BL implementation (Rosenthal & Weitz, 2012). The impact of unsupportive staff will likely depend on the extent of BL implementation. For example, if only those who were keen on implementing BL were involved in piloting BL into a school, the potentially unsupportive staff would be mere onlookers, less likely to have a negative impact. However, if unsupportive staff are core

73

members of the BL implementing team, morale may be affected, but also design and implementation within courses. This could potentially lead to reduced BL quality, poor evaluation outcomes, and an end to further BL implementation.

The success of BL implementation can be improved with some forethought, planning, and perhaps some little tricks from the literature. Strong leadership is necessary to establish goals and expectations (Beaver, Hallar, Westmaas, & Englander, 2015; Christensen, Horn, & Staker, 2013; Parkes, Zaka, & Davis, 2011; Lynch et al, 2015; Lynch, 2012). School leaders need to be motivated to change and to succeed, especially in the initial implementation stages and sites. Rosenthal and Weitz (2012) found that having a *Product Champion* involved in developing and implementing BL into the school improved successfulness of the process. A product champion should be a motivated staff member who is excited to be involved and perhaps even lead the implementation process. The product champion(s) should be rewarded with, besides potential monetary rewards, time to implement aspects of course changes. All staff involved, however, require support and recognition for their effort (Beaver, Hallar, Westmaas, & Englander, 2015; Garrison & Vaughan, 2008; Vaughan, 2007). This includes access to professional development, but also time to develop and encouragement to progress. Good communication channels between staff involved and the use of sharable resources is also important and can reduce individual workload (Littlejohn & Pegler, 2006; Stacey & Gerbic, 2008; Tabor, 2007). If good morale and positive outcomes can be attained in the piloting stages, a cultural shift may take place. This will not only improve cultural readiness, but, in turn, management readiness and personnel readiness.

Any number of BL models could and probably would work in any institute (Moskal, Dziuban, & Hartman, 2013). However, they would require augmenting to fit the specific school culture and climate. Augmentation into a finely tuned educational model appropriate for the specific school is a process which will likely take years and a number of iterations. Questions then arise as to what does success look like and how is it measured? In fact, focussing too much on implementation and not enough on evaluation has been found to hinder the transition to BL (Sharpe et al., 2006). Data collection evaluating BL success should not be an afterthought (Moskal, Dziuban, & Hartman, 2013). Initially, the effectiveness of the BL model(s) implemented should be assessed. Over time, longitudinal data can be used to assess trends. Once the model(s) have been shown to be effective, refinement and adjustment should still continue in order improve the quality of the BL model(s). Quality data collection can be used to support implementation of BL in other courses and other schools, but it can also be used to objectively show improvements in student outcomes. This can then improve environmental readiness and potentially even financial readiness, if funding relies on positive evaluations.

Often the first stages of BL implementation, as suggested above, include a pilot class or classes (Christensen, Horn, & Staker, 2013). This can be done within an existing school using a sustaining innovation model or using a disruptive innovation model. Earlier in this review, the section on BL models described Station Rotation, Lab Rotation, and Flipped Classroom models as sustaining, based on work by Christensen, Horn, and Staker (2013). Any one of these models could be implemented in a class with no effect on the rest of the school and without the need for extra or different staff. With permission from the principal, some planning and content development, and a few minor changes to the classroom (technology permitting), the Station Rotation model and the Flipped Classroom model could be implemented with ease. The Lab Rotation model would require the use of a computer lab external to the classroom.

The Flex, A La Carte, Enriched Virtual, and Individual Rotation models are considered disruptive innovations and require more effort to implement. However, Christensen, Horn, and Staker (2013) describe how they may be initially implemented into a school. To begin with, it is suggested that an autonomous team is assembled within the school to initiate the implementation. This team would require members with technical expertise to setup online systems. It is suggested to implement the disruptive innovation model(s) initially on a specific group of students, for example, struggling students who may require extra help or advanced students who my want to progress at a faster pace. At this stage, the model(s) should be adjusted and refined until it is effective. Once the model(s) is consistent and effective, it can be expanded to other courses in the school. Because the disruptive innovation models require funding, environment, and staff changes, it is important to plan and design for long term goals and commit to the project. When considering implementation into a number of schools, Beaver et al. (2015) identify that implementation of BL can successfully be introduced initially into whole schools, however, beginning with fewer schools is recommended. Whether the BL model being implemented is disruptive or sustaining, initial implementation with a small group can equip a group of teacher and administrators with BL knowledge, establish a framework for further development, and allow for adjustments from lessons learned for larger-scaled implementation (Michigan Virtual University, n.d.). Successful piloting of BL using a small group should improve content readiness and technical readiness.

Regardless of extent of BL implementation and BL models included, there are a number of early considerations to be made (Moskal, Dziuban, & Hartman, 2013). First of all, goals and objectives need to be identified. These might be at an institutional level (e.g. cost-cutting, increasing prestige), a faculty level (e.g. professional development, innovative teaching), and/or at a student level (improved learning outcomes, increased access and flexibility). Identification of goals at all three of these levels is preferable.

Another consideration is the capacity of the educational organisation to design and implement BL courses successfully (Moskal, Dziuban, & Hartman, 2013). How will staff be supported? Who will design the online content? Will there be a BL support unit to coordinate the implementation or will each department have their own? Questions of who will oversee the implementation are also necessary. Both top-down approaches (leader and management designed) and bottom-up approaches (teacher designed) are viable strategies (Beaver, Hallar, Westmaas, & Englander, 2015). An external BL designer may also be considered to aid in the transition by conducting professional development of staff and collaborating with staff on BL content design.

Terminology used for the different elements of BL also need to be developed and defined (Moskal, Dziuban, & Hartman, 2013). As discussed in the definition section, there is no consensus on terminology relating the BL. However, having clear operational definitions within the school will aid in professional development and communication among staff and students. What is the overall project to be known as? What terminology will be used to describe the technologies being implemented? Are various BL models being implemented? If so, what are their names?

Initial implementation can be rife with technical issues and an adjustment period for both teachers and students is likely (Poon, 2013; Weiss, Maser, Oliver, Parker, & Stallings, 2014). Technical support delivery needs to be considered (Moskal, Dziuban, & Hartman, 2013). This support can be outsourced or internal to the school. Students and teachers should have access to technical support. Continued assessment of what technology is available within the school, what it is capable of doing, and whether it is adequate is also recommended (Beaver, Hallar, Westmaas, & Englander, 2015). There is also a necessity for reliable infrastructure. Online content and the LMS needs to be readily available and reliable for students and staff to access at any time. Having backup plans to allow for continued teaching in the case of connectivity issues can alleviate tension, however, frequent and extended interruptions will have negative effects on outcomes and morale. The infrastructure must be able to handle the demand, leading to improved technical readiness.

Depending on the extent of BL implementation, policy development may require legal advice. Examples include, issues concerning workload increases or sharing, recognition for works completed, and who retains intellectual property. It is best to have policies developed early to cover these concerns.

Considerations of funding have been briefly touched on, but it is very important to figure out a clear budget for setup costs and the ongoing costs associated with BL. This may cover hardware purchases, software licensing, and cost of specialised staff. Of course there also may be savings on, for example, reduced F2F time required, reduced teacher workload due to an efficient LMS, and the use of paraprofessionals. In fact, BL can often have overall reduced costs over time (Moskal, Dziuban, & Hartman, 2013; Rosenthal & Weitz, 2012). Budgeting with foresight can save future costs. It may be helpful to reframe BL implementation as an investment rather than an expense.

Once the big picture considerations have been addressed, a similar process should commence in addressing the considerations of incorporating BL into courses (Inman, Wright, & Hartman, 2010). The course objectives need to be identified. The BL elements, or learning environments, then need to be decided upon based on the course objectives, but also dependent on the grade level. Different grades will benefit from different models of BL

(Michigan Virtual University, n.d.). Gradually increasing online content is considered best practice (Shana, 2009). An example is described by Staker and Horn (2012) of the Station Rotation model successfully being incorporated into a kindergarten class. Students in this class had minimal access to online content in a supervised in-class station for short periods throughout each day. Gradual increases in online content over K-12 grade levels can build independent and self-directed learning skills. Considerations of technology required for the BL elements then need to be addressed. Further course design and implementation considerations will vary substantially between grade levels, between subjects, and between schools. One thing, however, remains the same. The success of a BL course is dependent upon good planning and design (Jimoyiannis, Tsiotakis, Roussinos, & Siorenta, 2013; Lim et al., 2008; McNaught, Lam, & Cheng, 2012; Means et al., 2013; Sharpe et al., 2006). Learner readiness may need to be developed in the initial stages of implementation with technical and other forms of support (Abas, Kaur, & Harun, 2005).

Implementing BL into a school, when done correctly, is not a quick and easy process. It takes much planning and support. A motivated and innovative team, given the opportunity, can improve student outcomes while reducing school expenses with BL. This, however, involves plenty of planning, designing, implementing, evaluating, adjusting and refining (Powell, Rabbitt, & Kennedy, 2014). It also requires perseverance "toward ambitious, long-term educational and professional goals" (Powell, Rabbitt, & Kennedy, 2014, p. 10).

Limitations and Gaps in the Research

The limitations and gaps in the K-12 BL literature are vast (Bernard et al., 2009, 2014; Kassner, 2013; Means et al., 2009; Means et al., 2013; Skrypnyk et al., 2015; Tamim et al.,

2011). There are issues surrounding research design, the description of the implemented BL model, dissemination of findings, and, of course, a lack of the research actually occurring. This section will be used to highlight some of the specifics of these gaps and limitations. This is not intended to harshly criticise those who have conducted research in the field, but to aid forging a way forward in order to improve student outcomes when using BL. In the end, this should be about the students, not about the researchers.

The first concern to be addressed is the lack of research actually being performed. This goes against a common suggestion made in the literature: maintain ongoing evaluation of the implemented BL (Department of Education and Early Childhood Development, 2012; iNACOL, 2011; Moskal, Dziuban, & Hartman, 2013; Powell, Rabbitt, & Kennedy, 2014; Sharpe et al., 2006). Of course, the evaluation may be taking place, just not being disseminated, but this is not beneficial to BL development. One issue with performing research in a school setting is that the cycle of school sessions slows research (Means et al., 2013). Designing, implementing, and evaluating BL models and elements in the real world takes time. However, if the statistics on the number of students in BL education are true (Allen & Seamen, 2013; Horn & Staker, 2011; Skrypnyk et al., 2015), there are many opportunities for research either being wasted, or just not being disseminated. Also, if the suggestion of constant evaluation and refinement was followed, over time there would be longitudinal data to assess; another area lacking in BL research (Means, Toyama, Murphy, & Baki, 2013).

When a school implements BL, they are collecting data whether they are aware of it or not. That is, a BL model is incorporated into a course, the course is run, and students are graded on their outcomes. The model may then be adjusted, the course is run again, and the outcomes are recorded. A few minor tweaks to this already existing system, the writing up of a report, and the findings can be disseminated to the world. If more schools were to slightly adapt their current system to disseminate their outcomes, the BL phenomenon would advance at a much faster pace. Some may state that teachers are already overworked and have limited time and capacity to conduct this research. However, because the underlying data collection is already in place, one person or a small group could easily oversee the process and allow teachers to do very little more than they are already doing. Regardless of school staff motivation, outside help may be required for quality, detailed research (Sharpe et al. 2006). This outside help may come in the form of researchers from a nearby university, who are often very interested in real-world data.

There are a number of elements that are required in quality research. In this instance we are referring to quantitative research. Qualitative research has its place, usually in exploring and building theory, but there is always the issue of subjectivity; subjectivity in data collection and subjectivity in analysis. Quantitative research, on the other hand, can be used to objectively measure phenomena. Quantitative research needs to conform to standards, however, in order to be considered of good quality. For example, the use of a control group is ideal. A control group (e.g. an existing model) is used as a comparison to the experimental group (e.g. a new model). In order to keep the control and experimental groups similar, participants are usually randomly allocated to one or the other. It is important to try to eliminate differences in conditions besides those being assessed. This can be difficult in some BL research because it is suggested (e.g. Jimoyiannis et al., 2013; Sharpe et al., 2006) not to merely add online components to a traditional class, but to develop a BL course based on pedagogical reasons and theory. However, keeping as many elements constant as possible is ideal. Another important inclusion is a pre-treatment test of both groups. That is, both the control and experimental groups should be tested on their knowledge of the course topic and/or other variables of interest (e.g. satisfaction). There should ideally be no significant difference between the groups before the BL is implemented, but if there are, these can be statistically controlled for. These research design elements should allow for a comparison, not only of the final student outcomes, but of the difference in improvement between the group conditions.

There is enough literature to suggest that BL, if designed and implemented correctly, is beneficial to student outcomes (Jimoyiannis et al., 2013; Lim et al., 2008; McNaught, Lam, & Cheng, 2012; Means et al., 2013; Sharpe et al., 2006). Once a BL has been successfully implemented into a course, the next stage of research involves assessing new additions, redesigns, or refinement within the model (Bernard et al., 2014; Bernard et al., 2009; Tamim et al., 2011). For example, if a station rotation model has been incorporated into a kindergarten class and has been found to improve student outcomes, the next step may be to include a new automated guidance tool to assess its effect on student outcomes. In this case, the control group would participate in the existing station rotation model, while the experimental group would include the station rotation model, but with the automated guidance tool incorporated. This way, it is possible to assess which elements can improve student outcomes in a particular class.

Of course redesigns and refinement should be based on pedagogy and/or theory...of course. Of the most frequently cited BL resources, only 13% were found to use empirical research to refine a theory or build on a model (Halverson et al., 2014). If there is to be serious progress in BL research, this needs to change. Education has a long history of theory which will still be relevant in BL. Building on existing theories and models can help to give research direction; something currently lacking in the burgeoning field of BL.

Much of the literature surrounding online education and BL is based on perceptions, not empirical research (Barbour & Reeves, 2009). Less than one third of the most cited BL resources used inferential statistics (Halverson, Graham, Spring, Drysdale, & Henrie, 2014). More research needs to include how student learning is affected, even if the main focus of a paper is on teacher or student perceptions. It is no use for a BL course to make students and teachers feel good if academic achievements of students are being negatively affected. Considering that students are being graded on the course anyway (i.e. data is being collected), this shouldn't be too much to ask.

Another recurring issue within the literature, is that the BL models being implemented are not being described in full. Thus, readers are left with only a vague notion of what the BL involved (Sosa, Berger, Saw, & Mary, 2011). The BL model should be described in enough detail for the reader to be able to replicate it. Just mentioning that a discussion board was used, or that online content was made available is not enough. How was the discussion board being used? What was included in the online content? Disseminating research which includes vague methods drastically reduces its usefulness.

As can be seen from this section, there is a lot to be desired in BL research. It is a relatively new field, but steps can definitely be taken to hasten progress within the field. In a nut shell, this includes recording data from all BL implementation (especially student outcome data), having a group (or at the very least pre-implementation data) to compare results to, clearly describing exactly what has been implemented, and disseminating the findings. K-12 research in BL in particular requires good quality, quantitative studies to allow for any chance of inferring causation of BL elements. The diversity of design models, each with limited supporting research, hinders the progress of BL as a whole (Halverson et al., 2014). This can be seen in an inability to effectively communicate on the subject, which is just too vast and varied to conceptualise easily. The development and refinement of new and existing theory is necessary to hasten progress in BL research and to improve student outcomes in BL, but this can only be realized via the performance of high quality research and reporting.

Conclusions Drawn from the Literature

Blended learning (BL) is not tangible. It is not a single thing which will always be implemented in the same way or have the same outcome when it is implemented. BL is a term which allows us to communicate about a vast range of teaching strategies. Perhaps a better term would be *Modern Education*. Education will never go back to being a teacher standing in front of a class, forcing students to copy what they write on a black board...we hope. Digital technology will continue to grow in the classroom. Lifestyle, practicality, and circumstance will potentially increase the proportion of education being offsite and online. Pedagogy needs to adapt to these inevitable changes. It matters little what we call it. What does matter is how effective and efficient education is.

BL has been found to have a positive effect on student outcomes...overall. It is this 'overall' which needs to be highlighted to the readers. Sometimes BL has been found to have negative effects on student outcomes (e.g. Figlio, Rush, & Yin, 2013; Joyce et al., 2014; Kwak, Menezes, & Sherwood, 2015; Reasons, Valadares, & Slavkin, 2005). Poor outcomes in BL are often a function of students not being ready for BL (e.g. Lueken & Ritter, 2015), teachers not being confident or motivated to use technology in the classroom (e.g. Weiß & Bader, 2010), or simply because technology was thrown into the classroom as an afterthought (e.g. Kwak, Menezes, & Sherwood, 2015). Most studies have found that the implementation of BL has had a positive effect on student outcomes (e.g. Means et al.,

2013). This, however, may be a function of BL being novel to otherwise bored student or that BL often merely adds extra content, extra time for study, and extra means of interaction. What is BL if not all these things? BL is a construct that encompasses such a wide variety of elements that at the same time it can be good and bad; depending on planning, design, and implementation. Overall, however, BL has been found to positively affect education.

Enough research and meta-analyses have been performed to show that BL, under the right conditions, can lead to better student outcomes than traditional or solely online education (Bernard et al., 2014; Means et al., 2013; Tamim et al., 2011). This is not where we leave it though; this is only the beginning. Now we need to identify which of the elements work under which conditions. We need to stop trying to show that BL, the all-encompassing construct, is good or bad. We need to change our view from the macro, BL as a whole, down to the micro, specific BL elements. The time has now come to identify the specifics of what makes BL effective, and what can make it more effective. BL is a humungous entity which is yet to be fully harnessed. A systematic approach to researching BL is necessary to convert a dishevelled literature into an age of enlightenment for modern education.

High quality research should be conducted in all grades, in all subjects, within and between schools. This should be encouraged and made more efficient. For example, permission for the use of student data should be signed off by parents at the beginning of each year or even when being enrolled into the school. That is, it should be the standard that de-identified student data be used for research to improve educational strategies; it is, after all, already being collected. Research also needs to be carried out on all aspects of BL; from implementation, to teacher professional development, to student engagement and achievement. Research should be performed whether BL implementation is happening at a classroom level, at a school level, or across schools. Every aspect of BL implementation should include an element of data collection; both micro and macro level studies should be incorporated into the process. This may, however, require external support from experienced researchers to maintain quality control. The outcomes then need to be disseminated, regardless of whether outcomes were successful or not.

The specifics of BL cannot be recommended here for two reasons: 1) there is not enough good research to make claims with confidence; 2) the appropriateness of specific BL elements will vary for each school. However, general recommendations can be made. Recommendations when implementing BL into a school include making sure the school is ready: environmentally; culturally; managerially; personnel-wise; learner-wise; financially; technically; and content-wise. This is especially important when implementing at a whole-school level. Short-term and long-term goals need to be identified, outcomes need to be continuously evaluated, and adjustments made where necessary. A product champion and a motivated team should be involved in the piloting stages to increase chances for success. Strong leadership is necessary to guide the process and staff need to be supported technically, emotionally, and financially as deemed appropriate.

The role of the teacher will change with BL implementation. They will not retain the central position in the classroom they previously may have had. Instead, they should guide students through content and allow them to develop their own learning journey. Teachers will need to develop technical skills, educational skills, communication skills, and ethical knowledge. Some of this will carry-over from traditional teaching styles, but some aspects will need professional development. BL should be used to professionally develop teachers to be ready for BL. This will allow for the introduction of content, but will also give teachers practical skills in using BL tools and give teachers an awareness of the student point of view in BL. Teachers' extra workload then needs to be acknowledged and rewarded.

Many BL models have been developed; both sustaining (not requiring major changes to facilities or staff) and disrupting (requiring changes in facilities and staff). However, until a number of quality longitudinal studies have been carried out, the debate of which model(s) and what blend(s) are best is conjecture. Until best practices are developed, implementation of BL will need to be planned, evaluated, and adapted to suit the school, students, staff, parents, and community.

Regardless of reasons for implementing BL into a school or course, a major overall goal should be an improvement in student outcomes. Well-designed BL courses and well-prepared students will lead to increased student engagement and improved student achievement. Technology should be incorporated into a course based on pedagogy and clearly identified objectives. Self-regulated learning should be built into the curriculum and students should have more control over their learning journey. Self-regulated learning skills are especially important if students will have reduced F2F time over their K-12 education. Also, although F2F time can be substantially reduced over the K-12 years, it should not be entirely removed.

It is hoped that this literature review has provided a picture of the state of BL at this time, instruction for those pursuing BL implementation, and direction for future BL research. Limited quality research on K-12 BL exists, so recommendations here have been generalised, in some cases, from tertiary-level BL and purely online education. For this reason, caution should be taken when following these recommendations, and, as has been suggested throughout this paper, outcomes should be continuously evaluated and designs should be adjusted as required.

Epilogue: What are the Implications for Teachers and Schools?

The implications for teachers and schools as society transitions from a 'knowledge society' (OECD, 1996) into the 'networked society' (Dirckinck-Holmfeld, 2016; Vom Brocke, 2016) are significant. The social impact of advances in new information and technologies, including Artificial Intelligence, Deep Learning, data mining, and robotics are emerging (Brynjolfsson & McAfee, 2014). However, what society is encountering is only the beginning. We are almost certainly at the bottom of the diffusion of innovation "S curve". Ongoing and accelerating technological innovations will generate even larger seismic shifts in the global flows of people, ideas, services, goods, finance, and information (Brynjolfsson, McAfee, & Spence, 2014; Christensen, Horn, & Johnson, 2011; Manyika, Bughin, Lund, Nottebohm, Poulter, Jauch, & Ramaswamy, 2014; OECD, 2013).

This significant impact is especially so for those who have been maintaining industrial age-inspired elements of schooling. The reality is that in many cases this investment in the status quo, including a reliance of standardized testing to measure school performance, will make the disruption experienced in the future even more confronting. It has been pointed out in previous chapters that the social and technological changes represents a significant departure from the era of schooling in which most teachers were raised, completed their university qualifications, and enjoyed successful careers (Hargreaves & Fullan, 2012; Lynch, 2012; Lynch et al., 2015).

Preparing students for a context we are only, in many cases, speculating about, poses a wicked problem for practitioners and policy makers. In the first instance, the capabilities necessary to thrive in the new economy described briefly above go beyond what traditional schooling has previously offered students. In addition, the need for schooling to better address the individual learning needs of students, rather than taking the 'shoot to the middle' approach of the industrial age 'factory school', is paramount. The continued 'sorting' of students on narrow academic indicators brings with it an unacceptable cost to a nation's human capital and economic prosperity.

However, we do know enough to act now and this final chapter is a call to arms and an optimistic view of what we should be doing now. Closing the gap between 'knowing' and 'doing' (Pfeffer & Sutton, 2000) requires purposeful action on behalf of the students by everyone associated with the teaching profession.

Taking action has implications for policy makers, school leader, and teachers, but it is the practitioners that need to act since innovation is nearly always ahead of policy development. It is true that having the macro level setting correct can facilitate change and improvement, but policy set around the short political cycles in many economies may not be responsive enough. It can also be argued that large bureaucracies, like education systems, are unable to incubate the innovation, entrepreneurship, and agility now necessary. Moving away from the BL research literature, this chapter outlines three considerations that school leaders and teachers can make to focus their intervention and action. These three strategies are concerned with the leadership required, the new collaborative mindset required of the profession, and a rethinking of the professional learning constructs in schools for both teachers and school leadership.

Although in a book about Blended Learning, these three strategies apply equally to schooling generally as the 'bigger picture' for teachers and school leaders to prepare students for the changing world. The reference points for implementing a Blended Learning approach have been made in this book (Willis, Lynch, Yeigh, Smith, Provost, & Sell, 2017) and by other authors (Horn & Staker, 2015; Dziuban & Graham, 2013; Welker & Berardino, 2005). In summary, a different set of capabilities is required because to thrive in the future, our students also need a different set of capabilities (Paltasingh, 2012; Zhao, 2012).

The leadership required

For some time now, the profession has actioned school improvement agendas around the work of teachers. This is a defensible strategy as approximately forty percent of the variance in student performance is accounted for in what happens in the classroom (Dean, Hubbell, Pitler, & Stone,2012; Hattie, 2009; Marzano, 1998; Robinson, Hohepa, & Lloyd,

2009). Whilst much less variance is accounted for from the leadership of the school, approximately seven to ten percent, there is no example of a school's improvement of student outcomes, sustained high performance at school or system level, or significant educational innovation in the absence of quality leadership.

Research into the impact of leadership practices and behaviours on student outcomes is a narrow field, as most studies indicate an indirect impact. However, this is an area of research that is starting to clarify the work required by leaders to bring about student level outcomes. It is the school's principal, supported by the leadership team, who creates the organizational conditions to enable teachers to affect quality teaching (Marzano, Waters, & McNulty, 2005; Robinson et al., 2009).

Research at the University of Auckland (Robinson at al., 2009) offered a model that frames three capabilities against five dimensions or leadership actions. There are other examples in the literature, and national institutes have also developed leadership frameworks to inform research informed practice (AITSL, 2015; The General Teaching Council For Scotland, 2012). However the Robinson et al. (2009) model is a good example due to its simple but comprehensive framework to reference effective research informed leadership practices. The model identifies three capabilities: applying relevant knowledge; solving complex problems; and building relational trust. The five dimensions, arguably the most recognized and cited part of the study due to the meta-analysis and the published effect sizes, are:

- Establishing goals and expectations (ES= 0.42)
- Resourcing strategically (ES= 0.31)
- Ensuring quality teaching (ES = 0.42)
- Leading teacher learning and development (ES = 0.84)
- Ensuring an orderly and safe environment (ES = 0.27)

In the context of a rapidly changing world, the leadership capabilities become paramount. As an example, little can be achieved in a school in the absence of high levels of relational trust. The building of professional capital relies strongly on the school leaders' ability to build and maintain relational trust (Hargreaves & Fullan, 2012). The complexity and unpredictability of problems that school leaders face also demands processes and professional capacities, and the application of educational knowledge.

Two of the of the dimensions in the Robinson et al. (2012) model also stand out in the adoption of a Blended Learning approach: establishing goals and expectations; and leading teacher learning and development. The professional learning dimension will be discussed in more detail in a later section of this chapter. Being clear about the strategic direction of the school and the way in which teachers are to undertake this work is best accomplished by a core set of organisational values and norms (Robinson et al., 2009). In a complex and quickly changing world, one that has been described as volatile, uncertain, complex, and ambiguous, providing the workforce with clarity about the work to be done becomes a highly important role of the school leader (Bennett & Lemoine, 2014). The clarity necessary about the purpose of the school, and what it is trying to achieve for the students, is articulated in organisational literature, including by Sinek (2017), and also in the BL literature (Beaver, Hallar, Westmaas, & Englander, 2015; Christensen, Horn, & Staker, 2013; Parkes, Zaka, & Davis, 2011).

Facilitating change and improvement in the school is built around the existing workforce, primarily teachers, being prepared for the change agenda; this is no different in the incorporation of eLearning into a school (Abas, Kaur, and Harun, 2005). Schiemann (2012) explains this as optimizing the organisation's 'talent', and recent application of this work in the school setting is promising school leaders some key insights into how 'ready' the school is for the change agenda (Lynch & Smith, 2016). The three component of an organisation's talent is Alignment, Capability, and Engagement; again reinforcing the relevance of goals, expectations, and professional learning.

A collaborative mindset is required

Collaboration is increasingly being identified as essential in the school reform and improvement agenda. New and emerging industries are already leveraging collaborative mindsets and practices to help drive innovation and growth. An example of how new industries collaborate can be found in an examination of the independent (indie) gaming development community. Developers often work in teams on complex projects, from various locations including across national and international borders, accessing individual creative and technical expertise to collaboratively build a game. 'The Arcade', established in 2013 by the Game Developers Association of Australia (The Arcade, N.D.), is a converted Melbourne warehouse that today houses thirty separate businesses consisting of approximately eighty people. What makes this workplace worthy of reference by school leaders, is the way these separate businesses and their people support and learn from each other, despite the traditional mindset being of being 'in competition'. These businesses share ideas, provide expert assistance to each other, and even offer labour for each other during peak times or when deadlines are to be met. 'Feedback Friday' provides the opportunity to have a game tested by what other industries would consider the 'competition', who provide valuable feedback that ultimately improves that game. The level of collaboration is surpassed by the shared celebration when a game is brought to market and is a success.

Certainly this is a very different environment to a school, and the rate of failure in terms of games that are not successful would be unacceptable in the teaching profession. However, school leaders and teachers will benefit by considering the opportunities such collaborative practices might provide for schools and teachers generally, and student learning outcomes specifically. Collecting and disseminating evidence of successes and failures in BL implementation, as suggested in a previous section, is an important aspect of collaboration; opening communication channels between schools and their leaders.

Collaboration in education is articulated in a range of initiatives since 'communities of practice' entered the lexicon in the early 1990s. Since then, Professional Learning Communities, Teacher Learning Communities, collaborative inquiry initiatives, and the many iterations of these, have found their place in the theory and practice of schooling. As collaboration in this sense is located in a professional learning and capacity development frame, it will be addressed in a following section.

Collaboration at the organisational level demands building of networks and partnerships with individuals and organisations. This 'collective leadership' (Petrie, 2014) creates access to skills and knowledge that a single manager, or organisation, might not possess. The notion of social capital being the avenue of raising professional capital means connections between teachers, schools and their leaders, and others in organisations, including universities, is a requirement in a complex world (Hargreaves & Fullan, 2012; Leana & Pil, 2006). The bottom line is that problems are becoming too complex for individual leaders to solve.

Educational change has also too often been driven by government policy or the education system - at the 'macro' level. Macro level approaches rely on impacting the human capital in schools (Hargreaves & Fullan, 2012) by implementing external measures to bring about change (Hattie, 2015b; Munby & Fullan, 2016). This 'top down' change, in which government and education systems use policy, rules, mandated practices, and rewards and punishments, fails to consider motivation for change. Such policy leavers only go so far because they diminish the motivation of the most important people in the change process – school leaders and teachers. The evidence indicates that, since the mid-nineteen eighties, developing human capital through external accountability has not achieved the desired results (Hattie, 2015b; Munby & Fullan, 2016; Hargreaves & Fullan, 2012).

Change at the micro level, located at the individual school leader, is an important element of sustainable change, but also has its limitations. It is haphazard, as this 'bottom up change' leaves leaders to their own device and is inconsistent when looking for improvement across schools and systems. It produces an environment in which some, with the right communities, leadership capabilities, teachers, resources, and social capital, thrive. Others are maintained by the 'power of the status quo' by either coasting on the strength of socio-economic privilege, or continuing to fail students because of their disadvantage and indifference of addressing the discrimination of low expectations.

Munby and Fullan (2016) ask, "if top-down change does not work, and bottom-up change is not coherent or too variable, what is the solution?" Key to a new approach to school improvement, is the collaboration between teachers and school leaders within *and across* schools – in the 'meso' or 'middle' level.

Typically the 'meso' relates to the community or organization, and in this discussion the school or network of schools that sits between the micro, the individual school or school leader, and the macro, the educational system or policy environment.

Jensen et al. (2016) cite work being undertaken in British Columbia that uses an inquiry approach to facilitate professional learning and exchange across the school system. These 'Networks of Inquiry and Innovation' (NOII), operating independently in the space between schools and the education system, build professional capital and facilitate professional learning through the exchange of ideas, sharing of outcomes, and changing of mindsets. Timberley, Kaser, and Halbert (2014) argue that "new approaches to learning are necessary and that new designs for learning are required" and that this is achieved through "a disciplined approach to collaborative inquiry" (p. 4). They contend that "innovation floats on a sea of inquiry and that curiosity is a driver for change" (Timberley, Kaser, & Halbert, 2014, p. 4).

Making the time for this type of collaboration in a school setting is a leadership challenge in many schooling contexts. This has been identified in a study that determined that, in the higher performing education jurisdictions, teachers had less student contact time and, thus, increased capacity to collaborate with their teaching colleagues (Jensen, Hunter, Sonnemann, & Cooper, 2014; Mourshed, Chijioke, & Barber, 2010).

A rethinking of Professional Learning

Within the school, the most powerful avenue for developing talent is 'high quality collaborative, job focused professional development amongst teachers and school leaders' (Barber & Mourshed, 2009, p. 30). In 2014, AITSL published 'Global trends in professional learning and performance & development.' Five trends were identified in the report, from fifty international examples, that AITSL suggest have implications for schools and those responsible for developing the capabilities of school staff (AITSL, 2014, p. 7).

The report suggests professional learning should: be embedded within organisational culture and practice; provide 'intensive, holistic experiences that challenge beliefs and values, and radically alters practice'; and contain 'problem-solving processes that require deep understanding of and engagement' for those involved.

The professional learning 'market' across the world is being driven increasingly by financial considerations. The implications for school leaders and teachers is about a return on investment – how will this potential learning opportunity impact on outcomes for staff, schools, and ultimately students?

The growth in this market is not surprising. The expanding service sector is a known phenomenon in the 'knowledge economy' and it would be naive to think professional learning is not a commodity to be sold. However, in a pragmatic sense, the problem manifests for school leaders in a number of ways. One is full email inboxes with messages selling the next conference, workshop, program, book, or webinar. A second way it impacts on school leaders is the need to navigate the claims and assurances, and locate opportunities that align to their personal and strategic needs.

It should be noted that the need for individuals to have greater 'agency' and 'design' of their professional development is also supported by AITSL (2014, p. 16). Indeed, research into employee motivation identifies autonomy, mastery, and purpose as powerful motivators for change, improvement, and performance (Pink, 2009). It follows then that teachers will perform at their best when offered the professional autonomy of making decision about their work in a way that will help them master the complex nature of that work and make a positive difference for their students.

Autonomy does not mean a laissez-faire approach to the profession; which teaching knowledge, skills, and practices are important should be informed by educational research. Being led by educational research is critical and school leaders must not be distracted by the 'next shiny thing' of professional learning. Programs must be underpinned by the best current research evidence and be delivering outcomes to participants and students.

Hargreaves (2003) explains that school leaders need to develop the wisdom of knowing when external expertise is required in a professional learning agenda, and when it is more beneficial to access the knowledge within the school. Jensen, Sonnemann, Roberts-Hull, and Hunter (2016), through a review of the literature, outlined seven features of effective professional learning for teachers. These are that effective professional learning:

- Offers extended opportunities for learning over a period of time
- Engages teachers in real practice-related content
- Is focused on how to better support student learning
- Is in undertaken in collaboration with other teachers
- Involves active inquiry, challenge and critique
- Has external input, and
- Has coherence with current research (Jensen et al., 2016, pp. 32-33).

As previously outlined, of the five leadership dimensions Robinson et al. (2009) highlighted in their meta-analysis, 'promoting and participating in teacher learning and development,' with an effect size of 0.84, was the most impactful. School leaders must be involved alongside teachers in the professional learning agenda. Designing professional learning experiences around the findings of Jensen et al. (2016) and Robinson et al. (2009) reinforces that a school must focus on a one or two key capacity building agendas, embed this in the daily work of the school over time, and balance the accessing of external input with the mobilisation of internal expertise. Adding to do this, feedback, data analysis, coaching, mentoring, and feedback mechanisms should underpin the professional learning in a school (Lynch et al., 2015).

Feedback has been clearly established as important in the building of teaching capabilities (Hattie, 2019, 2015a). In this schooling context, *feedback* is defined in the literature as "information provided by an agent regarding aspects of one's performance or understanding" (Hattie & Timperley, 2007 p.81). The scope of information in a school setting includes analysis of student learning data (Sharratt & Fullan, 2012), formal and informal teacher observations, and appraisals.

Coaching, and the closely related mentoring, are additional opportunities for teachers and school leaders to receive feedback on their performance that should be built into professional learning agenda.

Taken together, the coupling of mentoring with coaching and feedback for effects on teachers is designed to "help individuals to improve their performance in various domains, and to enhance their personal effectiveness, personal development, and personal growth" (Hamlin, Ellinger, & Beattie, 2008, p. 291).

This is because "truly effective managers and managerial leaders are those who embed effective coaching into the heart of their management practice" (Hamlin et al., 2008, p. 326). Further, Cordingly and Buckler point out the "positive impact on both teacher and learner outcomes of mentoring and coaching, with the most important message being that the processes typically involve sustained collaboration, embedded in real-life learning contexts, and supported by specialists" (2012, p. 221). The addition of feedback provides objective parameters through which performance can be judged and remedial actions targeted and assessed for impact. Collaborative inquiry (Timperley, Halbert, & Kaser, 2012) and 'teacher as researcher' projects (Madden, Lynch, & Doe, 2015; Sell & Lynch, 2014), which are conceptualised, implemented, and evaluated in each teacher's respective classrooms, provide opportunity for professional learning that is consistent with the literature (for further information see: Lynch and Smith, 2012; Lynch and Madden, 2014; Lynch and Smith, 2016, 2007;2011;2012;2013; Lynch and Yeigh, 2013).

.

Professional learning and leadership development

In an environment in which the importance of leadership being distributed within the organisation is accepted, separating 'leadership' from the positional power of school roles may be seen as a shortcoming. Harris (2014) illustrates how a distributed leadership model builds social capital and enhances a professional learning community and, in turn, builds capacity for school improvement. While the following section is framed around leadership development, the point needs to be made that it applies to leadership in the broad sense. That is, it may apply to teachers, principals, and other school leaders.

A 2015 Mckinsey report states that, while over ninety percent of CEOs were planning to increase investment in leadership development in the coming years as it is seen as the 'single most important human-capital issue their organizations face,' only forty-three percent are confident their investment will bear fruit (Feser, Mayol, & Srinivasan, 2015).

In a recent Centre for Creative Leadership white paper, four trends 'for the future' of leadership development are explored. These are 'more focus on vertical development, a transfer of greater developmental ownership to the individual, a greater focus on collective rather than individual leadership and a much greater focus on innovation in leadership development methods' (Petrie, 2014, p. 6). Petrie's premise is summed up in the statement, 'it's no longer a leadership challenge – it's a development challenge.' This signals a move from competencies, or what leadership looks like, to how to grow leadership mindsets.

The proposition is founded on the premise that an environment in which the work is becoming more complex and challenging, the skills leaders require have changed, and that more complex thinkers are needed, but that the methods we are currently using to develop leaders have not changed (Petrie, 2014 p.9).

An interesting aspect of Petrie's argument is the move to greater consideration of vertical development rather than the horizontal development focus of most current leadership programs. Horizontal development is about competencies and the development of new skills, abilities, and behaviours. There is, of course, knowledge school leaders possess that needs to be 'codified and transmitted' (Petrie, 2014, p.11), and it is important to framing development of these skills in others. However, in a complex world, Petrie suggests this is necessary but not sufficient.

Vertical development relates to personal 'stages of development' and how individuals make sense of their world. The wisdom that turning twenty-one means one is a fully developed adult is challenged with further 'steps' of cognitive development to be achieved. An individual is able to 'learn more, adapt faster, and generate more complex solutions than they could before' (Petrie, 2014, p. 12) through further cogitative development. Petrie argues that people with high levels of development perform better in complex environments and that the reason many leaders are feeling 'stressed, confused, and overwhelmed' is that most have not reached these higher cognitive levels.

'In terms of leadership, if you believe that the future will present leaders with an environment that is more complex, volatile, and unpredictable, you might also believe that those organizations who have more leaders at higher levels of development will have an important advantage over those that don't' (Petrie, 2014, p. 12).

Leadership development should also consider generic and transferable leadership competencies codified in the literature from the business world, if for no other reason than the enormous resources invested by this sector. An example is the 2015 Mckinsey project that identified a small subset of leadership behaviours that correlate to leadership success. They surveyed nearly two hundred thousand people and determined four types of behaviours accounted for 89 percent of the variance between strong and weak organisations. The four behaviours were: be supportive; operate with a strong results orientation; seek difference perspectives; and solve problems effectively (Fesser, Mayol, & Srinivasan, 2015).

Conclusion

This chapter outlined three considerations for the implementation of a change agenda suitable for adopting a Blended Learning approach in a school. In effect, this final chapter is an examination of evidence from the leadership and professional learning literature and a consideration of 'what does this mean' for teachers and school leaders.

To bring together ideas that schools can action, three final points are now made by way of a summary. Firstly, clarity and purpose about what the leadership is attempting to achieve in implementing a Blended Learning approach is the work of the school's leadership. The building of relational trust to foster stronger levels of professional capital is important in complex change agendas, and changing teacher practice is indeed complex work. Codifying how a Blended Learning approach is framed, that is, what it would look like when the elements are embedded in teacher practice, provides an important reference point for school leaders and teachers, and also contributes to the clarity around the school's strategic intent discussed earlier in this book. While Petrie's (2014) argument that vertical as well as horizontal development could also be considered, the initial priority is making clear the expectations of the change agenda.

Secondly, this work is to be underpinned by a mindset of collaboration. Fundamental to this is teachers collaborating at the level of planning and implementation of learning programs, informed by the analysis of student data, receiving feedback, including that from coaching and mentoring, and adjusting appropriate pedagogical interventions. School resourcing, including time to effectively collaborate, is therefore also required.

At the school level collaboration comes through partnerships formed in the development of specific professional learning programs and objective advice and feedback. The change agenda is enhanced by co-opting the expertise of a university, institute, or professional association, offering the school expertise it would otherwise not have access to. Such partnerships also ensure the balance between external and internal expertise can be facilitated.

And finally, the school's leadership will invest in a focused professional learning agenda, limited to one or two desired and specific outcomes. The focus areas should be given the time and resourcing necessary to support teacher learning that results in a change in teacher behaviour. The school's leadership must also be deeply involved in this learning so they are aware of the issues, problems, and the progress being made.

In a quickly changing world, monitoring the external environment in terms of technological and social changes will also be necessary. Technological advances and insights from new research require a level of agility and responsiveness. The profession of teaching now requires an informed understanding of what is happening in other sectors of the economy, and particularly those in which rapid technological advances are being made.

References

Abas, Z. W., Kaur, K., & Harun, H. (2005). *e-learning readiness in Malaysia 2004*. Ministry of Energy, Water and Communications, Malaysia and Open University Malaysia. Retrieved from https://www.academia.edu/1134811/E-Learning_readiness_in_malaysia?auto=download

AdvancePath Academics (n.d.). Blended Learning. Retrieved from http://www.advancepath.com/blendedLearning

AITSL. (2014). *Global Trends in professional learning and performance & development*. Melbourne: Educational Services Australia.

AITSL. (2015). *Australian professional standard for principals and the leadership profiles*. Melbourne: Educational Services Australia.

Allen, I. E., & Seaman, J. (2013). *Changing course: Ten Years of Tracking Online Education in the United States*. Babson Survey Research Group and Quahog Research Group. Retrieved from http://www.onlinelearningsurvey.com/reports/changingcourse.pdf

Allen, I. E., Seaman, J., & Garrett, R. (2007). Blending In: The Extent and Promise of Blended Education in the United States. Sloan Consortium. Retrieved from http://files.eric.ed.gov/fulltext/ED529930.pdf

Arbaugh, J. B. (2014). System, scholar or students? Which most influences online MBA course effectiveness? *Journal of Computer Assisted Learning, 30*(4), 349–362. http://doi.org/10.1111/jcal.12048

The Arcade Melbourne (N.D.). *The Arcade Melbourne*. Retrieved from http://thearcade.melbourne/

Arend, B. (2009). Encouraging Critical Thinking in Online Threaded Discussions. *The Journal of Educators Online, 6*(1), 1–23. Retrieved from http://files.eric.ed.gov/fulltext/EJ904064.pdf

Azevedo, R., & Cromley, J. G. (2004). Does Training on Self-Regulated Learning Facilitate Students' Learning With Hypermedia? *Journal of Educational Psychology, 96*(3), 523–535. https://doi.org/10.1037/0022-0663.96.3.523

Backlund, P., & Hendrix, M. (2013). Educational games-are they worth the effort? A literature survey of the effectiveness of serious games. In *Games and Virtual Worlds for Serious Applications, 2013 5th International Conference*. Retrieved from http://ieeexplore.ieee.org/xpls/abs_all.jsp?arnumber=6624226

Baig, I. (2015). A study of inverted classroom pedagogy in computer science teaching. *International Journal of Research Studies in Educational Technology, 4*(2), 19–30.

Barbour, M. K. (2012). Training teachers for a virtual school system: A call to action. *Creating Technology-Rich Teacher Education Programs: Key Issues*, 499–517. https://doi.org/10.4018/978-1-4666-4502-8.ch081

Barber, M. & Mourshed, M. (2009). *Shaping the future: How good education systems can become great in the decade ahead.* McKinsey & Company.

Barbour, M. K., & Reeves, T. C. (2009). The reality of virtual schools: A review of the literature. *Computers and Education, 52*(2), 402–416.

Bennett, N., & Lemoine, J. (2014). What VUCA really means for you. Harvard Business *Review, 92,* (1/2).

Beaver, J. K., Hallar, B., Westmaas, L., & Englander, K. (2015). *Blended Learning: Lessons from Best Practice Sites and the Philadelphia Context.* Retrieved from www.phillyeducationresearch.org.

Bernard, R. M., Abrami, P. C., Borokhovski, E., Wade, C. A., Tamim, R. M., Surkes, M. A., et al. (2009). A meta-analysis of three types of interaction treatments in distance education. Review of Educational Research, 79(3), 1243–1289. doi:10.3102/0034654309333844.

Bernard, R. M., Borokhovski, E., Schmid, R. F., Tamim, R. M., & Abrami, P. C. (2014). A meta-analysis of blended learning and technology use in higher education: From the general to the applied. *Journal of Computing in Higher Education,* 26, 87–122. http://dx.doi.org/10.1007/s12528-013- 9077-3

Blackmon, S. (2012). Outcomes of Chat and Discussion Board Use in Online Learning: A Research Synthesis. *Journal of Educators Online,* 9(2), 1–19. Retrieved from http://www.eric.ed.gov/ERICWebPortal/search/detailmini.jsp?_nfpb=true&_&ERICExtSearc h_SearchValue_0=EJ985399&ERICExtSearch_SearchType_0=no&accno=EJ985399

Bliuc, A. M., Ellis, R., Goodyear, P., & Piggott, L. (2010). Learning through face-to-face and online discussions: Associations between students' conceptions, approaches and academic performance in political science. *British Journal of Educational Technology, 41*(3), 512–524. http://doi.org/10.1111/j.1467-8535.2009.00966.x

Borup, J., Graham, C. R., & Davies, R. S. (2012). The Nature of adolescent learner interaction in a virtual high school setting. Journal of Computer Assisted Learning, 29(2), 153-167. doi: 10.1111/j.1365-2729.2012.00479.x

Brown, J. S., & Adler, R. P. (2008). Minds on Fire: Open Education, the Long Tail, and Learning 2.0. *EDUCAUSE Review, 43*(1), 16–32.

Brynjolfsson, E., & McAfee, A. (2014). *The second machine age: Work, progress, and prosperity in a time of brilliant technologies.* WW Norton & Company.

Brynjolfsson, E., McAfee, A., & Spence, M. (2014). New world order: Labor, capital, and ideas in the power law economy. *Foreign Affairs, 93*(4), 44-53.

Bujak, K. R., Radu, I., Catrambone, R., Macintyre, B., Zheng, R., & Golubski, G. (2013). A psychological perspective on augmented reality in the mathematics classroom. *Computers & Education, 68,* 536-544.

Cavanaugh, C., Gillan, K. J., Kromrey, J., Hess, M., & Blomeyer, R. (2004). *The Effects of Distance Education on K-12 Student Outcomes: A Meta-Analysis.* Learning Point Associates/North Central Regional Educational Laboratory (NCREL).

Chandra, V., & Lloyd, M. (2008). The methodological nettle: ICT and student achievement. *British Journal of Educational Technology*, *39*(6), 1087–1098. doi:10.1111/j.1467-8535.2007.00790.x

Chang, M. M. (2005). Applying Self-Regulated Learning Strategies in a Web-Based Instruction—An Investigation of Motivation Perception. *Computer Assisted Language Learning*, *18*(3), 217–230. https://doi.org/10.1080/09588220500178939

Cheung, W. S., Hew, K. F., & Ling Ng, C. S. (2008). Toward an Understanding of Why Students Contribute in Asynchronous Online Discussions. *Journal of Educational Computing Research*, *38*(1), 29–50. http://doi.org/10.2190/EC.38.1.b

Christensen, C. M., Horn, M. B., & Johnson, C. W. (2011). *Disrupting class: How disruptive innovation will change the way the world learns*. New York: McGraw-Hill Education.

Christensen, C., Horn, M., & Staker, H. (2013). *Is K-12 blended learning disruptive: An introduction of the theory of hybrids*. *Clayton Christensen Institute (May 2013)*. Retrieved from http://scholar.google.com/scholar?hl=en&btnG=Search&q=intitle:Is+K-12+Blended+Learning+Disruptive+?+An+introduction+of+the+theory+of+hybrids#0

Clark, K. R. (2015). The Effects of the Flipped Model of Instruction on Student Engagement and Performance in the Secondary Mathematics Classroom. *Journal of Educators Online*, *12*(1), 91–115. http://doi.org/3592584

Class, B., & Schneider, D. K. (2014). Design issues for technology-enhanced professional development. *Journal of Interactive Learning Reserach*, *25*(2), 161–186.

Cordingly, P., & Buckler, N. (2012). Mentoring and coaching for teacher's continuing professional development. . In S. Fletcher, Mullen, C. (Ed.), *SAGE Handbook of Mentoring and Coaching in Education* (pp. 215-227). London and New York: SAGE Publications.

Dabbagh, N., & Kitsantas, A. (2011). Personal Learning Environments, social media, and self-regulated learning: A natural formula for connecting formal and informal learning. *Internet and Higher Education*, *15*(1), 3–8. https://doi.org/10.1016/j.iheduc.2011.06.002

Davis, N., & Rose, R. (n.d.). *Professional Development for Virtual Schooling and Online Learning*. Retrieved from http://files.eric.ed.gov/fulltext/ED509632.pdf

Dean, C., Hubbell, E., Pitler, H., & Stone, B. (2012). *Classroom instruction that works* (2nd ed.). Alexandria, VA: ASCD.

Dede, C., Jass Ketelhut, D., Whitehouse, P., Breit, L., & McCloskey, E. M. (2009). A Research Agenda for Online Teacher Professional Development. *Journal of Teacher Education*, *60*(1), 8–19. http://doi.org/10.1177/0022487108327554

Dell, C. A., Low, C., & Wilker, J. F. (2010). Comparing Student Achievement in Online and Face-to-Face Class Formats. *Merlot Journal of Online Learning and Teaching*, *6*(1), 30–42.

Dengler, M. (2008). Classroom Active Learning Complemented by an Online Discussion Forum to Teach Sustainability. *Journal of Geography in Higher Education*, *32*(3), 481–494. http://doi.org/Doi 10.1080/03098260701514108

Department of Education and Early Childhood Development. (2012). *Blended Learning: A synthesis of research findings in Victoria education 2006-2011*. Melbourne, Victoria. Retrieved from www.education.vic.gov.au/researchinnovation/

DiPietro, M., Ferdig, R. E., Black, E. W., & Preston, M. (2008). Best Practices in teaching K-12 Online: Lessons learned from Michigan Virtual School teachers. *Journal of Interactive Online Learning*, 7(1), 10–35. Retrieved from www.ncolr.org/jiol

Dos, B. (2014). Developing and evaluating a blended learning course. *Anthropologist, 17*(1), 121–128.

Dziuban, C. D., Hartman, J. L., & Moskal, P. D. (2004). *Blended Learning. Research Bulletins* (Vol. 2004). http://doi.org/10.1111/j.1365-2923.2010.03653.x

Fesser, C., Mayol, F., & Srinivasan, R. (2015). *Decoding leadership: What really matters*. McKinsey Quaterly.

Figlio, D., Rush, M., & Yin, L. (2013). Is It Live or Is It Internet? Experimental Estimates for the Effects of Online Instruction on Student Learning. *Journal of Labor Economics, 31*, 763–84.

Florida TaxWatch. (2007). Final Report: A Comprehensive Assessment of Florida Virtual School. *Florida TaxWatch Center for Educational Performance and Accountability*. Retrieved from http://www.inacol.org/research/docs/FLVS_Final_Final_Report(10-15-07).pdf

Francescato, D., Porcelli, R., Mebane, M., Cuddetta, M., Klobas, J., & Renzi, P. (2006). Evaluation of the efficacy of collaborative learning in face-to-face and computer-supported university contexts. *Computers in Human Behavior, 22*(2), 163–176. http://doi.org/10.1016/j.chb.2005.03.001

Galy, E., Downey, C., & Johnson, J. (2011). The Effect of Using E-Learning Tools in Online and Campus-based Classrooms on Student Performance. *Journal of Information Technology Education, 10*, 209–230. Retrieved from http://proxygw.wrlc.org/login?url=http://search.ebscohost.com/login.aspx?direct=true&db=er ic&AN=EJ940902&site=eds-live&scope=site

Garrison, D. R., & Vaughan, N. D. (2008). *Blended learning in higher education: Framework, principles, and guidelines*. San Francisco, CA: Jossey-Bass.

The General Teaching Council For Scotland. (2012). *The standards for leaderhip and management: Supporting leadership and management development*. Edinburgh: GCT Scotland.

Gerard, L., Matuk, C., McElhaney, K., & Linn, M. C. (2015). Automated, adaptive guidance for K-12 education. *Educational Research Review, 15*, 41–58. http://doi.org/10.1016/j.edurev.2015.04.001

Graham, C. R. (2012). Emerging practice and research in blended learning. In M. G. Moore (Ed.), *Handbook of distance education* (3rd ed., pp. 333–350). New York, NY: Routledge.

Gros, B. (2016). The Dialogue Between Emerging Pedagogies and Emerging Technologies. In L. M. Blaschke & S. Hase (Eds.), *The Future of ubiquitous Computing* (pp. 3–23). https://doi.org/10.1007/978-3-662-47724-3_1

Halverson, L. R., Graham, C. R., Spring, K. J., Drysdale, J. S., & Henrie, C. R. (2014). A thematic analysis of the most highly cited scholarship in the first decade of blended learning research. *Internet and Higher Education, 20*, 20–34. https://doi.org/10.1016/j.iheduc.2013.09.004

Hamlin, R. G., Ellinger, A. E., & Beattie, R. S. (2008). The emergent "coaching industry": A wake-up call for HRD professionals. *Human Resource Development International, 11*, 287-305.

Hargreaves, A., & Fullan, M. (2012). *Professional capital: Transforming teaching in every school.* Toronto: Teachers College Press.

Hargreaves, D. H. (2003). *Education epidemic: Transforming secondary schools through innovation networks.* Demos.

Harms, C. M., Niederhauser, D. S., Davis, N. E., Roblyer, M. D., & Gilbert, S. B. (2006). Educating educators for virtual schooling: Communicating roles and responsibilities. The Electronic Journal of Communication, 16(1-2). Retrieved from http://ctlt.iastate.edu/~tegivs/TEGIVS/publications/ JP2007%20harms&niederhauser.pdf

Harris, A. (2014). *Distributed leadership Matters: Perspectives, practicalities, and potential.* Thousand Oaks, California: Corwin.

Hastie, M., Hung, I., Chen, N., & Kinshuk. (2010). A blended synchronous learning model for educational international collaboration. *Innovations in Education and Teaching International, 47*(1), 9–24. http://doi.org/10.1080/14703290903525812

Hattie, J. (2009). *Visible Learning: A synthesis of over 800 meta-analyses relating to achievement.* New York: Routledge.

Hattie, J. (2015a). *What works best in education: The politics of collaborative expertise.* London: Pearson.

Hattie, J. (2015b). *What doesn't work in education: The politics of distraction.* London: Pearson

Hattie, J., & Timperley, H. (2007). The power of feedback. *Review of Educational Research, 77*(1), 81-112. doi:10.3102/003465430298487

Heafner, T. L., & Friedman, A. M. (2008). Wikis and Constructivism in Secondary Social Studies: Fostering a Deeper Understanding. *Computers in the Schools, 25*(3-4), 288–302. doi:10.1080/07380560802371003

Hew, K. F., & Cheung, W. S. (2010). Use of three-dimensional (3-D) immersive virtual worlds in K-12 and higher education settings: A review of the research. *British Journal of Educational Technology, 41*(1), 33–55. http://doi.org/10.1111/j.1467-8535.2008.00900.x

Holker, B., Romeo, G., Henderson, M., Auld, G., Russell, G., Seah, W. T., & Fernando, A. (2008). *Exemplar Schools: Using Innovative Learning Technologies. Faculty of Education, Monash University.* Retrieved from http://www.deewr.gov.au/Schooling/DigitalEducationRevolution/Documents/exemplar_schools_report1.pdf

Holmberg, B. & Anderson, W. G. (2003). A theory of distance education based on empathy. In M. G. Moore (Eds.), *Handbook of distance education* (pp. 79–86). London: Lawrence Erlbaum.

Horn, M. B., & Staker, H. (2011). *The Rise of K-12 Blended Learning.* Retrieved from https://doi.org/10.1007/978-3-8349-9318-2_11

Horn, M. B., & Staker, H. (2015). *Blended: Using disruptive innovation to improve schools.* San Fransisco: Jossey-Bass.

Hudson, D. L., Whisenhunt, B. L., Shoptaugh, C. F., Visio, M. E., Cathey, C., & Rost, A. D. (2015). Change takes time: Understanding and responding to culture change in course redesign. *Scholarship of Teaching and Learning in Psychology, 1*(4), 255–268. http://doi.org/http://dx.doi.org/10.1037/stl0000043

INACOL. (2011). *National Standards for Quality Online Courses National Standards for Quality Online Courses (Version 2).* Retrieved from http://www.inacol.org/wp-content/uploads/2013/02/iNACOL_CourseStandards_2011.pdf

iNACOL. (2011). *National Standards for Quality Online Teaching.* Retrieved from http://www.cde.state.co.us/onlinelearning/download/NACOL_Standards_Quality_Online_Te aching.pdf

iNACOL. (2011). *The Online Learning Definitions Project. iNACOL.* Retrieved from http://www.inacol.org/research/docs/iNACOL_DefinitionsProject.pdf

iNACOL. (2013). *Research Agenda 2013-2018.* Retieved from http://www.inacol.org/wp-content/uploads/2015/02/iNACOL-Research-Agenda-October-2013.pdf

iNACOL. (2013). *RETHINK: Planning and designing for K-12 next generation learning.* Retrieved from http://www.educause.edu/library/resources/rethink-planning-and-designing-k-12-next-generation-learning

Inman, C., Wright, V. H., & Hartman, J. A. (2010). Use of Second Life in K-12 and Higher Education: A Review of Research. *Journal of Interactive Online Learning, 9*(1), 44–63.

Jensen, B., Hunter, J., Sonnemann, J. & Cooper, S. (2014). *Making time for great teaching.* Melbourne: Grattan Institute

Jensen, B., Sonnemann, J., Roberts-Hull, K. & Hunter, A. (2016). *Beyond PD: Teacher professional learning in high-performing system - Australian Edition.* (Appendixes) Washington DC: National Centre on Education and the Economy.

Jimoyiannis, A., Tsiotakis, P., Roussinos, D., & Siorenta, A. (2013). Preparing teachers to integrate web 2.0 in school practice: Toward a framework for pedagogy 2.0. *Australasian Journal of Educational Technology, 29*(2), 248–267. doi:10.1234/ajet.v29i2.157

Joyce, T.J., Crockett, S., Jaeger, D.A., Altindag, O., & O'Connell, S.D. (2014). *Does Classroom Time Matter? A Randomized Field Experiment of Hybrid and Traditional Lecture Formats in Economics.* Working Paper No. 20006, NBER. Retrieved from http://www.djaeger.org/research/wp/w20006.pdf

Junco, R., Elavsky, C. M., & Heiberger, G. (2013). Putting twitter to the test: Assessing outcomes for student collaboration, engagement and success. *British Journal of Educational Technology, 44*(2), 273–287. doi:10.1111/j.1467-8535.2012.01284.x

Kanuka, H., & Anderson, T. (1999). Using constructivism in technology-mediated learning: Constructing order out of the chaos in the literature. *Radical Pedagogy*, *1*(2). Retrieved from http://citeseerx.ist.psu.edu/viewdoc/download?doi=10.1.1.506.5182&rep=rep1&type=pdf

Kassner, L. (2013). *A Review of Literature: Mix It up with Blended Learning in K-12 Schools. Metropolitan Educatonal Research Consortum.* Retrieved from http://eric.ed.gov/?q=blended+learning+AND+%22literature+review%22&ft=on&ff1=subLit erature+Reviews&id=ED548381

Kim, C. M., Park, S. W., Cozart, J., & Lee, H. (2015). From motivation to engagement: The role of effort regulation of virtual high school students in mathematics courses. *Educational Technology and Society*, *18*(4). 261–272.

Kistow, B. (2011). Blended learning in higher education: A study of a graduate school of business. Trinidad and Tobago. *Caribbean Teaching Scholar*, *1*(2). 115–128.

Klisc, C., Mcgill, T., & Hobbs, V. (2012). The Effect of Instructor Information Provision on Critical Thinking in Students Using Asynchronous Online Discussion. *International Journal on E-Learning*, *11*(3), 247–266. Retrieved from http://www.editlib.org/p/34568/

Koedinger, K. R., & Aleven, V. (2007). Exploring the assistance dilemma in experiments with cognitive tutors. *Educational Psychology Review*, *19*(3), 239–264. http://doi.org/10.1007/s10648-007-9049-0

Koehler, M., Mishra, P., & Cain, W. (2013). What is technological pedagogical content knowledge (TPACK)? *Journal of Education*, *193*(3), 13–20. Retrieved from http://www.editlib.org/p/29544/?nl

Kwak, D. W., Menezes, F. M., & Sherwood, C. (2015). Assessing the Impact of Blended Learning on Student Performance. *Economic Record*, *91*(292), 91–106. doi:10.1111/1475-4932.12155

Lage, M. J., Platt, G. J., & Treglia, M. (2000). Inverting the Classroom: A Gateway to Creating an Inclusive Learning Environment. *The Journal of Economic Education*, *31*(1), 30–43. http://doi.org/10.1080/00220480009596759

Leana, C., & Pil, F. (2006). Social capital and organizational performance: Evidence from urban public schools. *Organization Science*, *17*(3), 353-366.

Leelawong, K., & Biswas, G. (2008). Designing Learning by Teaching Agents: The Betty's Brain System. *International Journal of Artificial Intelligence in Education*, *18*, 181–208. Retrieved from http://ijaied.org/pub/997/file/997_Biswas08.pdf

Lim, J., Kim, M., Chen, S. S., & Ryder, C. E. (2008). An Empirical Investigation of Student Achievement and Satisfaction in Different Learning Environments. *Journal of Instructional Psychology*, *35*(2), 113–120. http://doi.org/10.1093/oxfordhb/9780199934898.001.0001

Lim, D. H., Morris, M. L., & Kupritz, V. W. (2007). Online vs. blended learning: Differences in instructional outcomes and learner satisfaction. *Journal of Asynchronous Learning Networks*, *11*, 27–42. http://doi.org/184.168.109.199

Littlejohn, A., & Pegler, C. (2007). *Preparing for Blended e-Learning*. London: Routledge.

Liu, F., & Cavanaugh, C. (2011). High Enrolment Course Success Factors in Virtual School: Factors Influencing Student Academic Achievement. *International Journal on E-Learning, 10*(4), 393–418.   Retrieved   from https://acces.bibl.ulaval.ca/login?url=https://search.ebscohost.com/login.aspx?direct=true&db=eue&AN=527647771&lang=fr&site=ehost-live

Lou, S. J., Chen, N. C., Tsai, H. Y., Kuo-Hung, T., & Shih, R. C. (2012). Using blended creative teaching: Improving a teacher education course on designing materials for young children. *Australasian Journal of Educational Technology, 28*(5), 776–792.

Lowes, S. (2005, June). *Online teaching and classroom change: The impact of virtual high school on its teachers and their school.* A paper presented at the meeting of the North Central Regional Educational   Laboratory,   Chicago,   IL.   Retrieved   from http://citeseerx.ist.psu.edu/viewdoc/download?doi=10.1.1.94.6353&rep=rep1&type=pdf

Lueken, M., & Ritter, G., (2015). Value-added in a Virtual Learning Environment: An Evaluation of a Virtual Charter School. *Journal of Online Learning Research, 1*(3), 305–335.

Lynch, D., (2012). *Preparing Teachers in Times of Change: Teaching school, standards, new content and evidence*, Primrose Hall Publishing Group, Brisbane,

Lynch, D., Madden, J. & Doe, T., (2015). *Creating the Outstanding School.* Oxford Global Press: London.

Lynch, D. & Smith, R., (2016). Readiness for School Reform. *International Journal of Innovation, Creativity and Change, 2*(3). 1-12.

Lynch, D. and Madden, J. (2014) Enabling Teachers to Better Teach Through Engaging with Research. *International Journal for Cross-Disciplinary Subjects in Education.*

Lynch, D., & Smith, R. (2006). The learning management design process. In D. Lynch & R. Smith (Eds.). *The rise of the learning manager* (pp. 53-67). Frenchs Forest, NSW: Pearson Education Australia.

Lynch, D. & Smith, R. (2007). Australian schooling: What future?. In R. Smith, D. Lynch & B. A. Knight (Eds.), *Learning management: Transitioning teachers for national and international change.* Frenchs Forest, NSW: Pearson Education Australia.

Lynch, D. & Smith, R. (2011). *Designing the Classroom Curriculum in the Knowledge Age.* Sydney: AACLM Press.

Lynch, D. & Smith, R. (2012). *Assessing and Reporting the Classroom Curriculum in the Knowledge Age.* London: Primrose Hall.

Lynch, D. & Smith, R. (2013). The challenge of changing teacher education. In D. Lynch & T. Yeigh (Eds.), *Teacher education in Australia: Investigations into programming, practicum and partnership* (pp 27-40). Brisbane: Oxford Global Press.

McLoughlin, C., & Lee, M. J. W. (2010). Personalised and self regulated learning in the Web 2.0 era: International exemplars of innovative pedagogy using social software. *Australasian*

Journal of Educational Technology, 26(1), 28–43. http://doi.org/10.1523/JNEUROSCI.4255-09.2010

McNaught, C., Lam, P., & Cheng, K. F. (2012). Investigating relationships between features of learning designs and student learning outcomes. *Educational Technology Research and Development, 60*(2), 271–286. http://doi.org/10.1007/s11423-011-9226-1

Madden, J., Lynch, D., & Doe, T. (2015). *Teacher researchers: Creating the outstanding school.* On-line: Lulu.com.

Manyika, J., Bughin, J., Lund, S., Nottebohm, O., Poulter, D., Jauch, S., & Ramaswamy, S. (2014). *Global flows in a digital age: How trade, finance, people, and data connect the world economy.* Retrieved from www.mckinsey.com/mgi.

Marzano, R. J. (1998). *A theory-based meta-analysis of research on instruction.* Aurora, Col.: Mid-Continent Regional Educational Laboratory.

Marzano, R., Waters, T., & McNulty, B. (2005). *School leadership that works: From research to results.* Auroroa, CO: ASCD and McREL.

Means, B. Toyama, T., Murphy, R., & Baki, M. (2013). The effectiveness of online and blended learning: A meta-analysis of the empirical literature. *Teachers College Record, 115*(3), 1–47.

Means, B., Toyama, Y., Murphy, R., Baki, M., & Jones, K. (2009). *Evaluation of Evidence-Based Practices in Online Learning. U.S. Department of Education.* http://doi.org/10.1016/j.chb.2005.10.002

Mentzer, G., Cryan, J., & Teclehaimanot, B. (2007). Two Peas in a Pod? A Comparison of Face-to-Face and Web Based Classrooms. *Journal of Technology and Teacher Education, 15*(2), 233–246.

Merchant, Z., Goetz, E. T., Cifuentes, L., Keeney-Kennicutt, W., & Davis, T. J. (2014). Effectiveness of virtual reality-based instruction on students' learning outcomes in K-12 and higher education: A meta-analysis. *Computers and Education, 70,* 29–40. http://doi.org/10.1016/j.compedu.2013.07.033

Michigan Virtual University. (n.d.). *Planning Guide for Online and Blended Learning: Creating new models for student success.* Retrieved from https://micourses.org/resources/pdf/toolkit/MVU_RPT_PlanningGuide.pdf

Moore, M. G., & Kearsley, G. (2005). Distance education: A systems view (2nd ed.). Belmont, CA: Thompson/Wadsworth.

Mortera-Gutierrez, F. J. (2006). Faculty Best Practices Using Blended Learning in E-learning and Face-to-Face Instruction. *International Journal on ELearning, 5*(3), 313–337. Retrieved from http://www.uwex.edu/disted/conference/resource_library/proceedings/04_1082.pdf

Moskal, P., Dziuban, C., & Hartman, J. (2013). Blended learning: A dangerous idea? *Internet and Higher Education, 18,* 15–23. http://doi.org/10.1016/j.iheduc.2012.12.001

Mourshed, M., Chijioke, C., & Barber, M. (2010). *How the world's most improved school systems keep getting better.* London, McKinsey and Company.

Munby, S. & Fullan, M. (2016). *Inside-out and upside-down: How leading from the middle has the power to transform education systems*. Education Development Trust, Motion Leadership. Retrieved from http://www.michaelfullan.ca/wp-content/uploads/2016/03/EdDevTrust-Global-Dialogue-FINAL.pdf

O'Dwyer, L. M., Carey, R., & Kleiman, G. (2007). A study of the effectiveness of the Louisiana algebra I online course. *Journal of Research on Technology in Education, 39*(3), 289–306. doi:10.1080/15391523.2007.10782484

OECD. (1996). *The Knowledge-based Economy*. Retrieved from https://www.oecd.org/sti/sci-tech/1913021.pdf

OECD. (2013). *Development 2013: Industrial policies in a changing world*. OECD Publishing. Retrieved from http:dx.doi.org/10.1787/persp_glob_dev-2013-10-en

Paltasingh, T. (2012). Entrepreneurship education & culture of enterprise: Relevance & policy Issues. *Indian Journal of Industrial Relations, 48*(2), 233-246.

Park, Y. (2011). A Pedagogical Framework for Mobile Learning: Categorizing Educational Applications of Mobile Technologies into Four Types. *The International Review of Research in Open and Distributed Learning, 12*(2), 78-102. Retrieved from http://www.irrodl.org/index.php/irrodl/article/view/791/1699

Parkes, S., Zaka, P., & Davis, N. (2011). The first blended or hybrid online course in a New Zealand secondary school: A case study. *Computers in New Zealand Schools: Learning, Teaching, Technology, 23*(1), 1–30.

Petrie, N. (2014). *Future trends in leadership development*. Centre for Leadership development. Retrieved from http://insights.ccl.org/wp-content/uploads/2015/04/futureTrends.pdf

Partridge, H., Ponting, D., & McCay, M. (2011). *Good Practice Report: Blended Learning*. Retrieved from http://eprints.qut.edu.au/47566/1/47566.pdf

Pena-Shaff, J., & Altman, W. (2015). Student Interaction and Knowledge Construction in Case-Based Learning in Educational Psychology using Online Discussions: The Role of Structure. *Journal of Interactive Learning Research, 26*(3), 307–329.

Pereira, J. A., Pleguezuelos, E., Meri, A., Molina-Ros, A., Molina-Tomas, M. C., & Masdeu, C. (2007). Effectiveness of using blended learning strategies for teaching and learning human anatomy. *Medical Education, 41*(2), 189–195. http://doi.org/10.1111/j.1365-2929.2006.02672.x

Pfeffer, J. & Sutton, R.I. (2000). *The knowing-doing gap: How smart companies turn knowledge into action*. Boston: Harvard Business School Press.

Philadelphia Education Research Consortium. (2014). *Blended Learning: Defining Models and Examining Conditions to Support Implementation*. Retrieved from http://8rri53pm0cs22jk3vvqna1ub-wpengine.netdna-ssl.com/wp-content/uploads/2015/11/Blended-Learning-PERC-Research-Brief-September-2014.pdf

Picciano, A. G. (2009). Blending with purpose: The mutimodal model. *Journal of the Research Center for Educational Technology*, 5(1), 4–14. Retrieved from http://www.rcetj.org/index.php/rcetj/article/view/11/14

Picciano, A., Dziuban, C., & Graham, C. (2013). *Blended Learning Research Perspectives* (Vol. 2). Florence: Taylor and Francis.

Pink, D. H. (2009). *Drive: The surprising truth about what motivates us*. New York: Riverhead Books.

Poon, J. (2013). Blended learning: An institutional approach for enhancing students' learning experiences. *Journal of Online Learning and Teaching*, 9(2), 271–288.

Powell, A., Rabbitt, B., & Kennedy, K. (2014). *iNACOL Blended Learning Teacher Competency Framework*. Retrieved from https://www.inacol.org/wp-content/uploads/2014/10/iNACOL-Blended-Learning-Teacher-Competency-Framework.pdf

Precel, K., Eshet-Alkalai, Y., & Alberton, Y. (2009). Pedagogical and Design Aspects of a Blended Learning Course. *The International Review of Research in Open and Distributed Learning*, 10(2). Retrieved from http://www.irrodl.org/index.php/irrodl/article/view/618/1221

Puzziferro, M. (2008). Online Technologies Self-Efficacy and Self-Regulated Learning as Predictors of Final Grade and Satisfaction in College-Level Online Courses. *American Journal of Distance Education*, 22(2), 72–89. https://doi.org/10.1080/08923640802039024

Quakertown Community School District (n.d.). *Online Learning Academy*. Retrieved from http://www.qcsd.org/site/Default.aspx?PageID=6574

Reasons, S.G., Valadares, K., & Slavkin, M. (2005). Questioning the hybrid model: student outcomes in different course formats. *Journal of Asynchronous Learning Networks*, 9(1), 83–94.

Reyna, J. (2016). Bringing Knowledge to Life : Implementing E-learning Across the School of Education. *International Journal on E- Learning*, 15(1), 101–120.

Robinson, V., Hohepa, M., & Lloyd, C. (2009). *School leadership and student outcomes: Identifying what works and why*. Best Evidence Synthesis Iteration (BES). Wellington: Ministry of Education.

Rocketship (2015). *Blended learning*. Retrieved from http://www.rsed.org/Blended-Learning.cfm

Roscoe, D. D. (2012). Comparing Student Outcomes in Blended and Face-to-Face Courses. *Journal of Political Science Education*, 8(1), 1–19. http://doi.org/10.1080/15512169.2012.641413

Rosenthal, D., & Weitz, R. (2012). Large-course redesign via blended learning: A post-implementation assessment across institutions. *International Journal on E-Learning*, 11(2), 189–207. Retrieved from http://www.editlib.org.ezproxy1.lib.asu.edu/p/34062

Salomon, G. (2000). *E-moderating the key to teaching and learning online*. London: Kogan Page.

Schiemann, W.A. (2012). *The ACE advantage: How smart companies unleash talent for optimal performance*. Alexandria, VA: Society for Human Resource Management.

Schmid, R. F., Bernard, R. M., Borokhovski, E., Tamim, R. M., Abrami, P. C., Surkes, M. A., et al. (2014). The effects of technology use in postsecondary education: A meta-analysis of classroom applications. Computers & Education, 72, 271–291. doi:10.1016/j.compedu.2013.11.002.

Seaman, J., & Tinti-kane, H. (2013). *Social Media for Teaching and Learning. Pearson Learning Solutions and Babson Survey Research Group.* Retrieved from http://www.onlinelearningsurvey.com.

Sell, K., & Lynch, D. (2014). *The teacher as researcher: Case studies in educational research.* Tarragindi, Australia Oxford Global Press.

Shana, Z. (2009). Learning with technology: Using discussion forums to augment a traditional-style class. *Educational Technology and Society, 12*(3), 214–228.

Sharpe, R., Benfield, G., Roberts, G., & Francis, R. (2006). The undergraduate experience of blended e-learning: A review of UK literature and practice. *The Higher Education Academy,* (October), 1–103. Retrieved from http://www.heacademy.ac.uk/resources/detail/Teachingandresearch/Undergraduate_Experience

Sharratt, L., & Fullan, M. (2012). *Putting faces on the data: What great leaders do.* Corwin Press.

Shea, P., & Bidjerano, T. (2010). Learning presence: Towards a theory of self-efficacy, self-regulation, and the development of a communities of inquiry in online and blended learning environments. *Computers and Education, 55*(4), 1721–1731. https://doi.org/10.1016/j.compedu.2010.07.017

Shulman, L. S. (1986). Those Who Understand: Knowledge Growth in Teaching. *Educational Researcher, 15*(2), 4–14. http://doi.org/http://www.jstor.org/stable/1175860

Skrypnyk, O., Joksimović, S., Kovanović, V., Dawson, S, Gašević, D., & Siemens, G. (2015). The history and state of blended learning. In George Siemens, Dragan Gasevic, & Shane Dawson (2015). *Preparing for the digital university: A review of the history and current state of distance, blended, and online learning.* Retrieved from http://linkresearchlab.org/PreparingDigitalUniversity.pdf

Sosa, G. W., Berger, D. E., Saw, A. T., & Mary, J. C. (2011). Effectiveness of Computer-Assisted Instruction in Statistics: A Meta-Analysis. *Review of Educational Research, 81*(1), 97–128. https://doi.org/10.3102/0034654310378174

Spanjers, I. A. E., Könings, K. D., Leppink, J., Verstegen, D. M. L., de Jong, N., Czabanowska, K., & van Merriënboer, J. J. G. (2015). The promised land of blended learning: Quizzes as a moderator. *Educational Research Review, 15,* 59–74. http://doi.org/10.1016/j.edurev.2015.05.001

Stacey, E., & Gerbic, P. (2008). Success factors for blended learning. In R. Atkinson & C. McBeath (Eds.), *Hello! Where are you in the landscape of educational technology?* Proceedings of the 25th ASCILITE Conference (pp. 964-968). Melbourne, Australia: Deakin University. Retrieved from http://www.ascilite.org/conferences/melbourne08/procs/stacey.pdf

Strang, K. (2013). Cooperative Learning in Graduate Student Projects: Comparing Synchronous Versus Asynchronous Collaboration. *Journal of Interactive Learning Research, 24*(4), 447–464.

Tabor, S. (2007). Narrowing the distance: Implementing a hybrid learning model for information security education. *The Quarterly Review of Distance Education, 8*(1), 47-57.

Tamim, R. M., Bernard, R. M., Borokhovski, E., Abrami, P. C., & Schmid, R. F. (2011). What forty years of research says about the impact of technology on learning: A second-order meta-analysis and validation study. *Review of Educational Research, 81*(3), 4–28. doi:10.3102/0034654310393361.

Timperley, H., Kaser, L., & Halbert, J. (2014). *A framework for Transforming Learning in schools: Innovation and the spiral of inquiry.* East Melbourne: The Centre for Strategic Education.

Torrisi-Steele, G., & Drew, S. (2013). The literature landscape of blended learning in higher education: The need for better understanding of academic blended practice. *International Journal for Academic Development, 18*(4), 371–383. https://doi.org/10.1080/1360144X.2013.786720

Twigg, C. A. (2003). Improving learning and reducing costs - New models for online learning. *Educause, 38*(5), 28–38. http://doi.org/10.1016/j.ygeno.2009.08.012

Ümit Yapici, I., & Akbayin, H. (2012). The effect of blended learning model on high school students' biology achievement and on their attitudes towards the internet. *Turkish Online Journal of Educational Technology, 11*(2), 228–237.

Vajoczki, S., Watt, S., Marquis, N., & Holshausen, K. (2010). Podcasts: Are they an effective tool to enhance student learning? A Case Study. *Journal of Educational Multimedia and Hypermedia, 19*(3), 349–362.

VanLehn, K. (2011). The relative effectiveness of human tutoring, intelligent tutoring systems, and other tutoring systems. *Educational Psychologist, 46*(4), 197–221.

Vanourek, G. (2011). An (Updated) Primer on Virtual Charter Schools: Mapping the Electronic Frontier. *Issue Brief,* (September). Retrieved from http://www.connectionsacademy.com/Libraries/PDFs/200608_AuthorizingMatters.sflb.ashx

Vaughan, N. (2007). Perspectives on blended learning in higher education. *International Journal on E-Learning, 6*(1), 81–94.

Vom Brocke, J. (2016). Interview with Martin Petry on "Digital Innovation for the Networked Society". *Business & Information Systems Engineering, 58*(3), 239.

Wade-stein, D., & Kintsch, E. (2004). Summary Street: Interactive Computer Support for Writing. *Cognition and Instruction, 22*(3), 333–362. http://doi.org/DOI:10.1207/s1532690xci2203_3

Walne, M. B. (2012). *Emerging Blended-Learning Models and School Profiles.* Retrieved from http://www.edustart.org/wp-content/uploads/2012/10/Emerging+BL+Models+and+School+Profiles+FINAL+09.21.12.pdf

Watson, J., Murin, A., Vashaw, L., Gemin, B., Rapp, C., Canuel, J., … Stone, A. (2011). *Keeping pace with K-12 online learning*. Evergreen Education Group.

Watson, J. (2008). *Blended Learning : The Convergence of Online and Face-to-Face Education. Promising Practices In Online Learning*. http://doi.org/10.1016/j.aca.2006.05.012

Weiß S. & Bader H.J. (2010). How to Improve Media Literacy and Media Skills of Secondary School Teachers. In Martin Ebner & Mandy Schiefner, *Looking Toward the Future of Technology- Enhanced Education: Ubiquitous Learning and the Digital Native*. New York: Information Science Reference.

Welch, A. (2012). The Role of Primary Students and Parents in Virtual Schools. *Distance Learning, 12*(2), 33–37.

Welker, J., & Berardino, L. (2005). Blended learning: Understanding the middle ground between traditional classroom and fully online instruction. *Journal of Educational Technology Systems, 34*(1), 33-55. doi:10.2190/67FX-B7P8-PYUX-TDUP

Willis, R., Lynch, D., Yeigh, T., Smith, R., Provost, S., & Sell, K. (2017). *Towards a Strategic Blend in Education: A review of the blended learning*. London: Oxford Global Press.

Yeh, H., & Lahman, M. (2007). Pre-Service Teachers' Perceptions of Asynchronous Online Discussion on Blackboard. *The Qualitative Report, 12*(4), 680–704.

York, R. O. (2008). Comparing Three Modes of Instruction in a Graduate Social Work Program. *Journal of Social Work Education, 44*(2), 157–172. http://doi.org/10.5175/JSWE.2008.200700031

Zhao, Y. (2012). Flunking innovation and creativity. *The Phi Delta Kappan, 94*(1), 56-61.

Zimmerman, B. J. (2000). Attainment of self-regulation: A social cognitive perspective. In M. Boekaerts, P. Pintrich, & M. Zeidner (Eds.), *Self-regulation: Theory, research, and applications* (pp. 13–39). Orlando, FL: Academic Press.

Zimmerman, B. J., Bonner, S., & Kovach, R. (1996). *Developing self-regulated learners*. Washington, DC: American Psychological Association.